SPRING REVOLUTION IN MYANMAR
Songs, Symbols and Tattoos of Resistance

Nandita Haksar

Daraja Press

Published by

Daraja Press

https://darajapress.com

Wakefield, Quebec, Canada

ISBN 978-1-997742-13-5 (soft cover)

This book is available for sale worldwide except South Asia
where it is available from Aakar Books https://aakarbooks.com

Cover design: Min Min Han

Library and Archives Canada Cataloguing in Publication

Title: Spring revolution in Myanmar : songs, symbols and tattoos of resistance /
Nandita Haksar.
Names: Haksar, Nandita, 1954- author
Description: International edition. | Includes bibliographical references.
Identifiers: Canadiana 20250325179 | ISBN 9781997742135 (softcover)
Subjects: LCSH: Burmese literature—21st century—History and criticism. | LCSH: Politics
and literature—Burma—History—21st century. | LCSH: Burma—History—Coup d'état,
2021—Literature and the coup. | LCSH: Burma—Politics and government—1988- | LCSH:
Burma—In literature.
Classification: LCC PL3979 .H35 2025 | DDC 895/.809358591054—dc23

Contents

Timeline of Military Rule in Myanmar

1948: Burma wins her independence with U Nu as prime minister.

1962: U Nu is ousted in a military coup led by Gen Ne Win. Ne Win abolishes the federal system and inaugurates "the Burmese Way to Socialism"; bans independent newspapers.

1974: A new constitution comes into effect, transferring power from the armed forces to a People's Assembly headed by Ne Win and other former military leaders.

1982: A law designating people of non-indigenous background as "associate citizens" comes into effect, barring such people from public office.

1988: National Uprising; thousands of people are killed in anti-government riots. The State Law and Order Restoration Council (SLORC) is formed.

1989: SLORC declares martial law, arrests thousands of people, including the leader of the National League for Democracy, Daw Aung San Suu Kyi.

1989: SLORC changes the name of the country the "Socialist Republic of the Union of Burma" to the "Union of Myanmar" and the capital from Rangoon to Yangon.

1990: The National League for Democracy (NLD) wins a landslide victory in the general election, but the militry refuses to hand over power.

1990: Two Burmese student activists, including Soe

Myint hijack a Thai Airways plane and land in Kolkata to focus world attention on the plight of Burmese people and demand the release of Aung San Suu Kyi.

2003: Aung San Suu Kyi is released from house arrest, travels arround the city; there is an assassination attempt on her on 30 May at Depayin; she escapes but at least 70 supporters are massacred.

2004: The capital of Myanmar shifted from Yangon to Nay Pyi Taw.

2007 August: Saffron Revolution erupts is response to the hike in fuel prices.

2008 April: The military government publishes a proposed new constitution, which allocates a quarter of seats in parliament to the military and bans opposition leader Aung San Suu Kyi from holding office.

2008: Cyclone Nargis causes devastation in the Irrawady delta region but the junta refuses international humanitarian aid. In the midst of the relief work it holds a referendum in May on the new constitution

2010 November: NLD boycotts elections; the Union Solidarity and Development Party (USDP) claims a resounding victory in the first election in 20 years. The junta says the election marks the transition from military rule to a civilian democracy. Aung San Suu Kyi is released from house arrest.

2011: Thein Sin becomes President in March after the country's first election in 20 years in November 2010. Under his administration the government frees political detainees, embarks on peace deals with ethnic minority groups, relaxes media censorship and legalises trade unions.

2012: Aung San Suu Kyi wins a seat in the 2012 by-election, marking her first entry into Myanmar's parliament.

2015: General elections are held on 8 November with the NLD winning an overwhelming majority of seats in the combined national parliament.

2016: Aung San Suu Kyi become the State Counsellor of Myanmar on 6 April. The position is specifically created for her since the law forbids anyone with a foreign spouse to be President.

2016: The Myanmar army carries out systematic killings and rape Rohingya Muslims in Rakhine State; Aung San Suu Kyi establishes an Advisory Commission on Rakhine State chaired by former UN Secretary-General Kofi Annan with the aim to promote peace, reconciliation, and welfare in Rakhine State. Buddhist extremists condemn the commission as foreign internference.

2017: Commission submits its report; Myanmar military continue crackdown on Rohingyas forcing nearly 700,000 to flee their country.

2019: Aung San Suu Kyi appears before the ICJ; international community criticizes her for not condemning the military outright;

2020: The NLD claims a resounding victory in the parliamentary elections taking more votes than it did in 2015. Alleging irregularities, the USDP demands a rerun of the election and calls for military help to ensure fairness.

2021: On 1 February, the military imposes a state of emergency. Power is transferred to military chief Min Aung Hlaing. Aung San Suu Kyi and other senior government officials arrested in a series of early morning raids.

2021-2025: People across the country demand the release of Aung San Suu Kyi and the elected members of the Parliament. Ethnic armed groups and the majority Bamar community make alliances and launch armed resistance to the Myanmar regime. The people launch a civil disobedience movement—the Spring Revolution—calling for democracy, federalism and reconciliation between all ethnic groups and religious minorities for a real democratic, federal Myanmar where all communities feel they equally belong.

Prelude: Celebrating Spring in the Midst of Violence

Protesters have been placing floral tributes at locations where security forces have killed demonstrators as well as other public spots, to remember the hundreds who have died since the 1 February coup.

Organizers had called for tributes to be laid at pubic places in memory of "heroes who can't come home."

–Myanmar protesters hold 'flower protests'[1]

In 1948, after 124 years of British colonization, Burma became an independent Republic. It was a country full of promise, with rich cultural traditions and a vibrant media.

However, the promise of peace and progress was cut short when the military took control in 1962 and from then to today it has never really loosened its grip over the people and resources of the country.

Burma was isolated from the rest of the world and disappeared from the collective public imagination of the international community.

There are books which give more formal histories of the wars and conflicts; of the geo-political issues underlying the civil war, the insurgencies and the drug wars. Everything you read about Myanmar is true: the military coups, the devastating natural disasters and ethnic conflicts.

However, what you do not often read about is the resilience of the peoples of Burma, their histories of resistance to military rule and the cultural expressions of that resistance. We do not hear the voices of the people, the men, women and children who are living through war, conflict, natural disaster, but still find the strength and courage to resist even while facing arrests, long detentions and even execution.

The people have resisted through strikes, protests and armed struggles. Each time, the military has crushed the people in brutal crackdowns. There was a brief period starting in 2011 when the military allowed a short-lived experiment with democracy. This was the period when the National League for Democracy led by Daw Aung San Suu Kyi shared power with the military. This period from 2011 to 2020 was the time when a new generation of Burmese grew up—they were tech savvy and had tasted freedom and they could dream of a good future for themselves.

In the November 2020 elections the National League for Democracy once again won and there was a glimmer of hope that the people would see their country return to democracy and the task of rebuilding the country could begin in right earnest; they hoped they could live in an open and free society.

If the National League for Democracy came to power they could repeal the 2008 Constitution, passed during a rigged referendum in the aftermath of Cyclone Nargis. This Constitution guaranteed the military 25 per cent of the seats in parliament. The rigged elections in 2010 further allowed them to consolidate the political field to their advantage. Everyone hoped that this would all change and Burma could have a new democratic, federal constitution.

However, these hopes were dashed when on 1 February 2021 the junta staged a coup and arrested and imprisoned the elected members of parliament, including Daw Aung San Suu Kyi.

This time the repression has been even more brutal. But

this time the resistance too has been long and sustained. For the first time in the history of Myanmar the armies of the ethnic minorities such as the Karens, Kachins, Shans have united with the armed groups of the majority community, the Bamar. The armed resistance is supported by the civil disobedience movement or the CDM. Trade unions, health workers, teachers, bureaucrats, students, bank staff—every section of the people are a part of the pro-democracy movement. That the armed resistance to the junta is largely crowd funded by the Burmese diaspora, makes it a unique movement. It has succeeded in liberating 50 per cent of the territory.

In the midst of this bitter conflict there are also various forms of cultural resistance. Commanders of armed units are writing poetry and protestors singing songs banned by the military. The military junta is lampooned on Facebook pages and people are tattooing their bodies with political symbols of resistance.

The protestors have called their resistance a Spring Revolution.

The Spring Revolution is a celebration of myriad forms of resistance in the form of poems, songs, cartoons and yes, tattoos. It is also the first time that social media and the internet have been used as powerful instruments for resistance.

This book is unashamedly a celebration of the spirit of the Burmese people, the majority Barmans and the ethnic nationalities and religious minorities. It includes a first-hand account of one Burmese activist from Monywa who has lived through it all, got arrested, been in prison several times, and is now a refugee in India. Living in exile, with images of his friends killed and others in detention, his act of resistance has been tattooing the milestones of the resistance on his body.

The people of Monywa have been carrying on their civil disobedience from the first days of the coup of 1 February 2021. Dozens of people have been killed, including the famous poet, Zaw Win, in violent crackdowns. Because their protest movement has endured in the face of extreme violence, young resistance leaders proudly call their hometown *'sauk kyaw tin Monywa'* (f***ing stubborn Monywa).

The military has banned songs, imprisoned poets, tortured leaders and executed writers. The daily life of the people in Myanmar is hell with massive displacement and thousands living in refugee camps. Wars and natural disasters have left people without homes, food and water but it has not been able to destroy their hope for a better future.

Resistance to the Myanmar military can be found in the poems and songs written by political prisoners and by commanders of ethnic armed groups. Writers and poets, cartoonists and tattoo artists continue their resistance from refugee camps, inside dark cells and from secret hideouts. Independent media, despite the bans, continues to broadcast from the jungles.

The Spring Revolution continues to blossom in the midst of armed resistance to brutal military violence. Many have had the words "Spring Revolution" tattooed on their bodies to remind them of their love of their cause and their commitment to uphold it at all costs.

This book is a tribute to the courage, confidence and spirit of resistance and resilience of the Burmese people.

NOTE

1. https://www.dw.com/en/myanmar-protesters-hold-flower-protests-to-honor-dead/a-57085367

1

Military Rule Begins in 1962[1]

It's OK. Never mind. Don't take it too seriously or
even personally. Shit happens.
Anyway, it's not your shit, is it?
It's not your problem that our country
will soon be
the world's unceremonious cemetery.
                                    –Zeyar Lynn, March 3, 2021[2]

Myanmar, officially the Republic of the Union of Myanmar, also known as Burma (the official name until 1989), is the largest country by area in mainland South East Asia with a population of about 55 million as of early 2024.

Burmese nationalism has always been very strong, with the country deciding not to join the Commonwealth because of strong anti-colonial, anti-British sentiment.

Democracy has been short-lived in the country. The military staged a coup in 1962; and from the time it came under military rule. Burma simply disappeared from the political imagination of the international community, isolated from the world behind a bamboo curtain.

In November 1990, two student activists hijacked a Thai Airways flight to Kolkata, India, with the sole intention of diverting international attention from the Gulf War to the military repression in their country. They risked life imprisonment just to get the media to turn its gaze on the plight of political prisoners, especially Daw Aung San Suu

Kyi, who was under house arrest. Incidentally, the Indian authorities found the hijackers to be "gentle and polite" and even allowed them to address a press conference.[3] The attention that the country got as a result of the incident was, however, short-lived.

The international media continues to ignore the situation in Myanmar, as do funding agencies and international humanitarian organizations. In part, this is because Myanmar has lower strategic significance to western powers and also because of the complexities within its borders. These complexities are rooted in the cultural diversity of the country.

Burma's Cultural Diversity

Myanmar is one of the most culturally and ethnically diverse countries in the world, with a recorded history going back centuries.

Migration is a crucial factor influencing the history of Myanmar. The country borders Bangladesh, China, India, Laos, and Thailand. India and Burma have relations going even before the advent of Buddhism.

There are eight major "national ethnic races" in Myanmar—Karen, Kachin, Kayah, Chin, Mon, Bamar, Rakhine and Shan—as well as 135 ethnic groups. The majority of the people, around 89.2 per cent, are Buddhist, but there are also Christians, Muslims, Hindus and those practising tribal religions. The Bamars constitute about two-thirds of the population. This multi-ethnic, multicultural, and multilingual country has a long history of attracting settlers from various backgrounds, creating a rich cultural mosaic of indigenous groups like the Shan, Karen, and Rakhine, alongside non-indigenous populations such as ethnic Chinese, Indians, and Anglo-Burmese.

The tensions and conflict between these ethnic groups come from resentment against Bamar chauvinism, which is integral to the military rule. These conflicts have been exacerbated by the impact of the divide-and-rule policy of the British, a policy that has continued under military rule.

A part of this divide-and-rule policy has been to give a fillip to Bamar chauvinism and suppress the voices of ethnic nationalities. From the beginning of army rule, the military began a "Burmanization" programme that resulted in the nationalization of the properties of businessmen, who were primarily of Indian and Chinese origin. It also served to sharpen the ethnic divide.

Next, the junta passed a law in 1982 disenfranchising sections of its own citizens. By creating a special legal position for 'natives', the law served to severely erode the citizenship rights of those deemed non-indigenous to Myanmar, particularly those with Chinese or South Asian ethnicity even as it extinguished the citizenship of the Rohingyas, the Muslims living in Rakhine state. And it is this citizenship law that the army used to undermine the pro-democracy movement when, in 2008, the military rulers changed the Constitution to prevent Aung San Suu Kyi from becoming the President of the country.

Diversity and the Challenge of Nation-Building

Burmese freedom fighters have for long tried to find a solution to the ethnic conflicts in their country. On 12 February 1947, following the end of the Second World War, national hero and interim President, General Aung San, managed to bring together in Panglong leaders from the Shan states, the Kachin hills, and the Chin hills to formally agree to a united Burma in return for federal authority and to force the British administration to grant all of Burma its freedom. The agreement did not, however, include all the ethnic groups and religious minorities in the country.

Even so, the Panglong Agreement was a watershed moment in Myanmar's history as it paved the way for

Burma's independence in January 1948. The agreement also gave some ethnic leaders the option of seceding from the union if they were unhappy with the new nation.

Sadly, neither did the promise of the Panglong Agreement see the light of day, nor did Aung San live to see Burma as a free nation. Months before it was to gain independence, Aung San was assassinated on 19 July 1947.

Even today, 12 February is celebrated as Union Day, a national holiday commemorating the signing and passage of the Panglong Agreement.

Democracy Under U Nu

The first Prime Minister of the Union of Burma was U Nu (1907-95), under the provisions of the 1947 Constitution of the Union of Burma, from 4 January 1948 to 12 June 1956, again from 28 February 1957 to 28 October 1958, and finally from 4 April 1960 to 2 March 1962. U Nu was a contemporary of India's first Prime Minister, Jawaharlal Nehru.

Hoping to unite the country, U Nu declared Theravada Buddhism as the state religion. With almost 90 per cent of its population following Buddhism, Myanmar is the most religious country in terms of the proportion of Buddhist monks in the population and the proportion of income spent on religion. Theravada Buddhism is practised in conjunction with the worship of *nats*, god-like spirits who can intercede in worldly affairs.

In the first decade after independence, even though the country was beginning to recover economically, it was politically unstable, with the ethnic minorities demanding their share in political power. Unable to deal with these demands, U Nu "invited" Army Chief of Staff General Ne Win (1911-2002) to take over the country for an interim period.

Military Rule and Resistance

On 2 March 1962, Ne Win, with 16 other senior military officers, staged a coup, arrested U Nu and placed Burma under a one-party "socialist" state. U Nu's daughter, Daw Than Than Nu, sought refuge in India and got a job at the All India Radio. She played an important role in supporting the 1988 Burmese activists who fled their country in the aftermath of the military crackdown.

On taking over the reins of power, Gen Ne Win arrested over 400 "communist sympathizers", of which 153 were deported to Coco Island in the Andaman Sea. The military justified its repression by presenting itself as the only institution which could keep the country together and keep the insurgents in check. In fact, what it seemed to be implementing was a divide-and-rule policy to ensure disunity among the ethnic nationalities so as to enable it to stay in power. As David Brenner points out: " The Burmese Communist Party (BCP), a former umbrella group that encompassed various ethnic armies, has proven how dangerous unity among the country's numerous ethnic rebel movements can be. Since the BCP's breakup in the late 1980s, the Tatmadaw (Burmese military) has done everything it can to single out individual armed groups. While it struck ceasefire deals with some, it concentrated its firepower on others."[4]

Gen Ne Win imposed military rule in the guise of socialism. In April 1962, the Revolutionary Council introduced the "Burmese Way to Socialism" and declared it Burma's state ideology. The Revolutionary Council then founded the Burma Socialist Programme Party (BSPP), and in 1974, Ne Win introduced a new Constitution and changed the name of the country from the Union of Burma to the Socialist Republic of the Union of Burma. All political parties were banned, as were student unions and trade unions.

A programme to Burmanize the population was launched to bring about the cultural assimilation of the ethnic minorities. However, this only led to further alienating them. As one Burmese writer explains: "Four types of Burmanization policies were employed in Myanmar to ensure the cultural assimilation of ethnic minority groups. First, Burmese was declared the official and virtually only language of instruction in all educational institutions. Secondly, the instruction of ethnic minority languages was denied and persecuted. Third, residential schools and universities for ethnic minority youths as young as 10 years old were established. Fourth, these institutions are controlled by the Ministry of Border Affairs instead of the Ministry of Education, under which all other public schools and universities operate."[5]

Many of the ethnic minorities took up arms to resist the Burmanization of their population.

Students Protest of 1962

The first to protest against the imposition of military rule disguised as socialism were the students of Rangoon University. Two days after Gen Ne Win took over, the All Burma Federation of Students' Union (ABFSU), University of Yangon Students' Union (UYSU), and Yangon District Students' Union (YDSU) took a stand against the coup, issuing a joint statement of condemnation.

In response, Ne Win's junta swiftly repealed the Rangoon University Act and dissolved the Rangoon University Council, which included respected professors and student representatives. They replaced it with a new University Council, comprised solely of generals and a handpicked rector, devoid of any independent voices from within the academic community

The military imposed stringent regulations on the campus hostels, transforming them into virtual prisons.

These rules restricted students' movements after dusk, confining them rigidly to their rooms, and imposed arbitrary limitations on eating hours in the dining room.

On 3 July 1962, students initiated protests within the confines of the Rangoon University campus, ignited by the enactment of prison-like hostel regulations and the unjust cancellation of exam results.

On 7 July, the police arrested several student leaders, including the All Burma Federation of Students' Union President Ko Thet. This act further exacerbated tensions. The police attempted to seize control of the Student Union building, using anti-riot batons and tear gas to disperse the students protesting the arbitrary arrests of their leaders.

In the early hours of 8 July 1962, students in the University of Rangoon awoke to a deafening explosion that ripped through the whole campus. The iconic Students' Union Building had been demolished, and an indelible piece of their shared heritage was lost forever.[6]

Even as this day is commemorated by students, subsequent protests have been for the restoration of the right of students to form unions and for academic freedom.

The next significant student protest was in 1974 over the funeral of U Thant (1909-74), a Burmese diplomat and the first Asian to be appointed United Nations Secretary General from 1961 to 1981. He was the first person to be awarded the Jawaharlal Nehru Award for International Understanding in 1965.

When U Thant died and his body was brought back to Rangoon, the military did not want to bury him with the honour he deserved. It was on this occasion that the students protested.

The account of those days is given by Hla Oo, who was then a first-year student at the Rangoon Institute of Technology. He posted this account on a website called New Mandala, hosted by the Australian National University.

An Eyewitness to the 1974 Student Protest[7]

Hla Oo writes:

"Believe it or not, our small group of about 50 students from the RIT's First Year Section-D unknowingly started the 1974 student uprising. The beginning of the so-called "U Thant Uprising" was the day I will never forget.... Then, in 1974, I was a first-year engineering student at the famous Soviet-built Rangoon Institute of Technology. (Bastard generals changed her name to some Yangon Technical University or some idiotic name later just to break her rebellious tradition.)

"We, the whole class of First Year Section-D, were in the lecture hall 1.... Suddenly, a couple of senior students burst into the lecture theatre and simply told us to get out and into the waiting buses just outside on the campus grounds. "Are you boys wearing htameins (women's sarong in Burmese) or what? Be a man and join us to protest the unfair treatment of our famous son of the land," that was their loud battle cry to jolt us out of the lecture hall and onto the buses.

"The reason for the protest was mad Ne Win's military government's refusal to build a memorial and tomb for the former UN General Secretary, the late U Thant.

"They were going to bury U Thant's body at Kyandaw Cemetery, and only later reluctantly agreed to let the general public show their respect at the grounds of Kyaikasan Racing Ground. The funeral casket was displayed on a stand, and the public was to queue up in many long lines under a brightly shining sun to give the last deserving respect to the famous son of our land.

"But on that particular day, General Ne Win made a serious mistake. He banned the public from the ground and allowed only the 3000-strong students of our RIT and the students from Rangoon Arts and Science University, RASU. So the senior students took the rare opportunity to stage the uprising without even letting us juniors know in advance.

"When we got there at the Kyaikasan Ground, we were somehow positioned right across the field from the stand where U Thant's coffin was. We could clearly see the silvery coloured casket and the fierce-looking throng of Military Police, civilian police, and many government officials.

"As we were patiently or unknowingly standing by our buses for our turn in line to reach the coffin, one senior student climbed onto the roof of one nearby bus and started giving us a rousing speech. That was the first time and only time I saw the famous student leader Tin Maung Oo close-up. He wasn't even from our RIT; he was from RASU, but he was clever enough to choose us as the spearhead of his carefully planned uprising. We RIT students are famous for our fighting spirits, as almost all of us are boys and young men.

"The summary of his rousing speech was that U Thant should be treated with more respect than Ne Win's thugs had so far shown, and we, the brave RIT students, had to take matters into our hands, so take the coffin, and build a deserving memorial for U Thant on the grounds of the historical Rangoon University Campus.

"Then he jumped down from the bus roof and started energetically attacking the about five-foot-tall iron-bar fence which stood between us and the stand. We just followed him, and the fence immediately collapsed, and the individual fence poles became the weaponry for the brutal assault on the security forces guarding the coffin.

"It was a blood bath on the manicured lawn. Many officials were either bashed or stabbed where they stood trying to stop the young students rushing towards them with murderous intent. I even saw a senior driving his pointed iron pole through the fat body of a police officer already flat on the ground. I didn't know how many exactly were killed there. Only a few days later, the government announced that the rioting students had killed at least 20 officials and injured many more that day.

"To make the story short, as we reached the coffin, a few seniors tried to lift the casket. I even gave a hand, but the coffin was so heavy it wouldn't budge. But many more hands joined in, and they eventually rigged a crude carrier, and we lifted the coffin onto our shoulders and brought it all the way to RASU.

"On the way, the marching band of rogue students were cheered and waved by many people standing by the sides of the roads as the news spread like wildfire all over Rangoon. They were giving us food, water, and cold drinks as if they could correctly guess that we were almost starving. I even managed to grab a boiled egg or two while I was still carrying U Thant's heavy coffin.

"It took us, the whole marching mob of at least 5,000, more than 4 or 5 hours to reach the RASU campus by nightfall. Once we got there, the seniors decided to lay the coffin inside the Grand Old Convocation Hall. We students were then organised by many seniors into various committees and sub-committees. Me and a group of my classmates ended up as the foot soldiers of a security sub-committee. We manned the now-closed iron gates of the big campus and had to check everyone coming or going through the gates.

"We didn't even go home, and the first few nights were like a fun-filled carnival, celebrating the rare moment of freedom. Every night, on the lawn right in front of the Convocation Hall, many seniors took turns to deliver rousing speeches about our uprising. We were on a high all the time there in our own campus fortress. We also didn't need to worry about our food as the whole of Rangoon had sent us truckloads of packed meals, Hta-Min-Dotes. The army and socialist government also left us alone for, I think, at least the first two or three weeks.

"Architectural students from our RIT designed the U Thant Memorial on the sacred ground of the old Student Union building, notoriously blown up with many students still inside by Ne Win's thugs just after the 1962 coup, and our Civil Engineering students built the grave. Later, U Thant's coffin was moved into the new tomb. It was a very rare moment of triumph and freedom for all of us inside the campus.

"The trouble started only later in the third week. The now-distressed government started sending their agents into the campus, and so many of them were caught by ever-alert students, as most of them were old or at least middle-aged men, who stood out among the young students.

"The ugly head of violence started showing up again among us. Every night, the security students with masks on their faces would bring out the already tortured and confessed spies into the large student crowd right in front of the RASU Convocation Hall and throw them to the violent mob waiting, ready for the blood. The brutal beating and bashing would go on every night as the situation became totally out of control from the student leaders inside the Convocation Hall. Some old men from the local government councils sent in as the informants were killed there on the spot.

"One night, the blood-thirsty crowd decided to go out of the campus to stage a violent attack on the Hle-Dan Police Station right outside of the RASU on the Prome Road. I followed them with a burning torch in my hand and ended up just outside the police station, which had a high fence. Their original plan was to torch the police station. As we gathered there many student leaders came out of the campus and tried to persuade the students to abandon the imminent attack on the police station and come back inside the campus. During their heated arguments, a few students bravely crossed the wide road and peered through the cracks in the timber-planked fence, and what I saw frightened me to the bone.

"Inside the large police compound were the truckloads of armed soldiers ready to fire. ....."

"As we didn't want to be facing their G3 rifles, once we knew the army presence, we came back inside, and that was the last night of our pathetic little rebellion against the ruthless military government. My tail tucked between my legs, I came back home early morning, and luckily, my uncle, who ran a ferry boat between Rangoon and our little Delta town, was at home, and he brought me back to his house as my mother had asked.

"That night, while I was peacefully asleep on the boat on my trip away from the troubles in Rangoon, the troops circled the RASU Campus watertight and violently attacked the rebelling students inside. Witnesses later recalled that, true to their well-known reputation, the battle-hardened soldiers killed many hundreds and captured thousands of students during that first night of the week-long brutal assault on the RASU Campus.

"According to many witnesses, that first night of assault was a bloodbath on the campus. The brave or naive students who wrongly believed that the UN flag would protect them and thus gathered at the new U Thant's grave were clubbed and bayoneted to death right there by the grave under the huge blue UN flag that accompanied the coffin all the way from UN Headquarters in New York. Many female students were rumoured to have been gang raped and later killed.....

"A few years later I ran into an old school friend who went to DSA and became a navy officer, and he told me the sordid tale of how they rid the bodies of slain students, of course after plying him with a bottle of scotch and plenty of satay-sticks at Chinatown.....the soldiers loaded the dead and dying from the scene of massacre onto the sand-filled Hino TE-11 trucks and, in the middle of the dark night, took them to the sand-filled naval barges waiting at the Than-Lhyet-Soon Naval Base. The bodies, many were still half-alive according to him, were then taken and dumped into the crocodile-infested waters by the sea.

"Later that night, I wept, remembering some of my friends had vanished forever after that uprising."

The Tatmadaw and the Junta

How was the Myanmar army able to impose military rule for so many decades?

The Tatmadaw is the official term for the armed forces of Myanmar. The Tatmadaw or the glorious one, had prestige because it was created by Burmese nationalists as an institution to fight against British colonialism (unlike the Indian army, which was created by the British as an instrument of imperialism).

The Tatmadaw was a creation of Gen Aung, considered the father of the nation. Gen Ne Win had taken part in the anti-colonial independence movement. These facts gave legitimacy to the Burmese army; it is only after the coup in 2021 that the people started referring to it as the junta.

The Tatmadaw justified its repression by presenting itself as the only institution which could keep the country together and control brewing insurgencies. What they did, however, was prevent the ethnic minorities from coming together by working out ceasefire deals with some rebel factions while, at the same time, supressing others.

Brenner writes:

"These ceasefire accords have mostly been accompanied by lucrative business concessions, which had another divide-and-rule effect. It sparked factionalising within armed ethnic groups, with some leaders getting rich and corrupt while others held on to their revolutionary principles. It also created an ever-widening divide between rebel organisations and local ethnic minority communities. While rebels turned into businessmen, exploiting their territories' natural resources in collaboration with the Tatmadaw and foreign companies, little wealth trickled down to the ordinary populace. These internal splits often created turmoil within ethnic armed groups and significantly weakened their military strength."

This divide and rule policy was bolstered by brute military force, with the ethnic minorities suffering harsher military repression than the Bamars. It took the 2021 coup to unite the Burman and ethnic nationalities in their fight to overthrow military rule. But the problem of ethnic division has only been suppressed, not resolved.

Economic Power

In addition to political control, the armed forces gained absolute economic control over the country. Under the Burmanization programme, the property and assets of the old business communities, Indians and Chinese, were nationalized, and much of it was distributed to the Burman community. Many of the Indians and Chinese were driven out of the country. Large parts of the economy were controlled by the military, and the families of the armed forces had special privileges, with access to special shops with imported goods.

It began with the armed forces being permitted to carry on business enterprises through the Defence Services Institute (DSI), which ran shops which sold imported goods, exempt from import duties and taxes.

A state-run enterprise, the Defence Services Institute was established in May 1961, under the 1961 Burma Economic Development Corporation Act, and it remained under military control. By 1963, the Burmese state formally took over banks as well as the production, distribution, import and export of commodities. BEDC was nationalized on 20 October 1963, as part of the implementation of the Burmese Way of Socialism. At the time of nationalization, BEDC consisted of 42 separate firms, including Burma Beverage Co., Mandalay Brewery and Distillery, along with various chemical and paint, pharmaceutical, poly-products, canning, shoes, garment manufacturers, book stores, housing and construction companies, fisheries, hardwood trading, hotel operators, and coal suppliers.

After the 2021 coup, a people's campaign to boycott goods made by military-controlled or owned corporations on the grounds that profits from these businesses were used to buy weapons, proved to be a success. One of the most successful campaigns has been the boycott of beer manufactured in corporations run by the junta.

In nearly three decades of rule by Gen Ne Win, Burma had accumulated a national debt of $3.5 billion, its foreign currency reserves had dwindled to between $20 million and $35 million, with debt service ratios standing at half of the national budget. Burma's economy had reached rock bottom.... the country was compelled to apply for the UN-afforded status of Least Developed Country (LDC) to get some badly needed relief.

Burma was designated a Least Developed Country (LDC) by the United Nations in 1987. The classification was part of an application process where the nation sought eligibility for international debt relief and additional financial aid from UN agencies.

Ban on Media

Burma's first constitution in 1947 guaranteed citizens the right to freely express their opinions and convictions. This gave Burma the reputation for having one of the freest presses in Asia. Before Burma came under military rule, there was a vibrant tradition of debates and discussions. At the time of independence, Burma had some 40 newspapers, but after the coup of 1962, newspapers critical of the government were closed down, editors were arrested, and by the seventies, only six remained—all of them controlled by the government.

Burma also had a strong literary tradition, but during military rule, censorship rules required that every book cover had to carry the following three lines: "Three Main National Causes are non-disintegration of the Union, non-disintegration of national solidarity, and the continuing maintenance of national sovereignty."

Poets have been an integral part of Burmese resistance and poetry the most censored form of literature. Illustrative of the junta's persecution of poets is the life of Tin Moe, one of the leading Burmese literary voices of the 21st century. It was U Tin Moe (1933-2007), who described the decades of army rule as "the years we did not see Dawn."

Saw Wai is another Burmese poet, a performance artist and a political activist. His controversial Valentine's Day verse "February 14" on the surface appears to be a romantic poem about the poet being jilted by a fashion model. A closer analysis, however, reveals a caustic political message as the first words of the lines, read vertically, declare "General Than Shwe is power crazy". He was arrested in 2008 for writing this poem.

Zeyar, Lynn's "The Ways of the Beards" evaded the scrutiny of the authorities, who concluded that the poem was simply a jocular disquisition on the phenomenon of beards. Nonetheless, the poem narrates the plight of the Chin, among the most persecuted and dispossessed ethnic groups in Myanmar

> Beards are looking for a chin-like word for a poem
> Beard is the war-torn town of the chin in civil war
> In the history of chin, beard is the defeated truth [...]
> Into the scene of the beard on trial, many myths are said to be trafficked in
> Probing at the word, the scar of the beard was found
> "Don't let the flag fall, Fight until only your beard remains" say the Bansai T-shirts [...]
> History will forgive my beard
> To install electric power all over the country,
> To establish beard power all over the land.

"The poem adeptly manipulates the anatomical association between beard and chin to centralise the extrajudicial killing, forced labour, unlawful detention, and mass displacement of Chin people. Beard is thus a multifaceted metonym for dictatorial power as well as Indigenous resistance," writer John Charles Ryan explains.[8]

Muang Day, poet and artist, described the extent of censorship in Burma in the generation after Tin Moe in an interview to the *Point* magazine:

> "Modernist poets from the generation before us got around the censors with ingenious metaphors. So, the censors came up with a long list of prohibited words: 'star', 'red', 'dawn',

'sun', and even the word 'she' [which could refer to Aung San Suu Kyi]. When we organized a performance art festival in 2008, the censors refused. 'We've never heard of performance art,' they said. 'So how can we censor it?' After some persuasion, six censors agreed to visit our studio, where one by one, our artists pitched them their ideas. One performance involved waving balloons and bursting them. The censors asked, 'What colour are the balloons?' 'Various colours,' we said. 'Don't use red,' they said. 'And don't burst them. That's anger, so we don't want it.' I wish I had videotaped the entire exchange. It was unreal."[9]

1988 National Uprising

Ne Win, like so many authoritarian leaders, printed money endlessly to finance his political goals. This caused money supply and inflation to rise uncontrollably, debilitating control over all economic sectors. Waves of nationalization broke the back of ethnic minorities as they were historically involved in small business, trade and finance.

The immediate cause of the national uprising of 8 August, 1988 (8.8.88) was the demonetizations in 1985 and 1987. The stated motivations were to curb money supply and to end profiteering and black marketing.

The 1987 demonetization had a devastating impact on the people; it wiped out their lifetime savings. Announced out of the blue by Ne Win on 5 September, apparently without the knowledge of senior officials, K25, K35 and K75 notes, issued just two years earlier, were pulled out of circulation. This time, no reason was given for the demonetization.

When schools reopened in late October 1987, underground groups in Rangoon and Mandalay produced dissident leaflets, which culminated in a series of bomb explosions in November. Police later received threatening letters from underground groups, who organized small protests around the university campus. In Mandalay, there were larger protests that involved monks and workers, with some burning government buildings and state businesses. Even though the Burmese state media did not report much on the protests, news of the protests quickly spread through the students' network

The protests, rallies and demonstrations continued, and on 8 August 1988, the protests took the shape of a national uprising. It is, therefore, known as the 8888 Uprising, and those students who participated in it call themselves the 88 generation.

The 8888 uprising started by students in Rangoon spread throughout the country. Hundreds of thousands of monks, children, university students, housewives, doctors and common people protested against the government. The uprising ended on 18 September after a bloody military coup by the State Law and Order Restoration Council (SLORC). Thousands of deaths have been attributed to the military during this uprising, while authorities in Burma put the figure at around 350 people killed.

It was during this national uprising that Aung San Suu Kyi emerged as a political leader and a national icon.

Daw Aung San Suu Kyi

Aung San Suu Kyi (b 1945) is the youngest child of General Aung San and Khin Kyi. She was only four years old when her father was assassinated. Her mother was the Burmese Ambassador to India, enabling Aung San Suu Kyi to live and study in India.

Aung San Suu Kyi went to Jesus and Mary School in New Delhi, and graduated from Lady Shri Ram College, a constituent college of the University of Delhi in New Delhi, with a degree in politics in 1964.

The college has kept alive the connection to the Burmese icon and in 2014, inaugurated the Aung San Suu Kyi Centre for Peace. The Centre is dedicated to fostering a culture of peace in the South Asian region.

Aung San Suu Kyi went to study at Oxford and, in 1972, married a historian Michael Aris (1947-99). They had two sons. She was living in the UK when her mother fell ill, forcing her to come back to her country of birth. This was 1988, the year of the national uprising. After her mother passed away, Aung San Suu Kyi did not return to her family. When her husband was diagnosed with terminal cancer, the junta did not give him a visa, and Aung San Suu Kyi, fearing that they would not allow her to re-enter the country even though she had a Burmese passport, did not go to visit him. Michael Aris died in the UK in 1999.

The students had brought Aung San Suu Kyi into the movement, and she soon took on the role of a political leader with the founding of a political party called the National League for Democracy (NLD) in 1988.

Thereafter, Aung San Suu Kyi and the NLD won every election in which they took part: 1990, 2012 (by-election), 2015 and 2020. Each time, the party won with a massive majority.

Despite the massive majority, the junta refused to hand over power to the elected members of Parliament in 1990. Instead, they put Aung San Suu Kyi under house arrest. From 1989 to 2010, Aung San Suu Kyi was under house arrest for 15 years. There were attempts on her life at Depayin in 2003 in which more than 70 NLD supporters were massacred, but she survived because of her driver's skills.

Aung San Suu Kyi burst into the international scene during the days of her first house arrest from 1989 to 1995. It was then that she became "symbolically omnipresent". Within the country, she was venerated almost like a female bodhisattva, a benevolent *nat*. Outside her country, she was portrayed as an icon of democracy, the Gandhi of Burma or the Jean d'Arc. Many awards were bestowed on her, including the Nobel Peace Prize in 1991.

Rohingya Persecution

In 2015, Aung San Suu Kyi won the elections but could not become President because of a provision under the Constitution promulgated by the junta in 2008.

As per Chapter 3, Article 59(f) of the 2008 Constitution, the President must be someone who "he himself, one of the parents, the spouse, one of the legitimate children or their spouses (do) not owe allegiance to a foreign power".

"[They shall] not be subject to a foreign power or citizen of a foreign country ... [or] be persons entitled to enjoy the rights and privileges of a subject of a foreign government or citizen of a foreign country."

Since Aung San Suu Kyi's husband and two sons were British citizens, she was disqualified from becoming President. However, in April 2016, a new post was created of State Counsellor of Myanmar, equivalent to a Prime Minister, for Aung San Suu Kyi.

It was during this time that there was a military crackdown on the Rohingyas living in Rakhine state. There had been attacks on Rohingyas earlier but the crackdown by the military in 2016 was particularly brutal.

Aung San Suu Kyi's Government established an Advisory Commission on the Rakhine State, chaired by Kofi Annan. The mandate of the Commission was "to analyse the situation in Rakhine State, identify factors contributing to violence and displacement, and develop recommendations in areas such as conflict prevention, humanitarian assistance, reconciliation, and development".

The Commission submitted its report in 2017. Buddhist extremists and nationalists in Myanmar strongly opposed the Kofi Annan-led Advisory Commission alleging that it amounted to inviting foreign interference in Myanmar's internal affairs.

The Buddhist extremist organizations including the 969

Movement and its successor, Ma Ba Tha, also known as the Patriotic Association of Myanmar criticized Aung San Suu Kyi and spread hatred against both the NLD and the Rohingyas calling them "illegal migrants".

The Rohingyas attacked some police stations and in August 2017 the Myanmar army backed by Buddhist extremist organizations began the crackdown on Rohingyas, forcing 645,000 Rohingyas to flee to other countries. Most fled to Bangladesh, resulting in the creation of the world's largest refugee camp there.

It is in this background we must see the international community's criticism of Aung San Suu Kyi's stand on the Rohingyas before the International Court of Justice.

In 2019, Gambia filed a case against Myanmar for the genocide of the Rohingyas before the International Criminal Court, and since Aung San Suu Kyi was the State Counsellor, she appeared on behalf of Myanmar. It should be remembered that she still did not have control over the army since 25 per cent of the seats in the Parliament were reserved for the military. As the State Counsellor, she accepted there was a serious problem in the Rakhine state but denied that it was a genocide. She said Myanmar should be allowed to deal with the sensitive issue in the way it thought best.

Aung San Suu Kyi stated that her government would take urgent measures to address the problem, particularly to control the spread of hate. However, the international community denounced her for not taking a stronger stand and condemning the military outright, without paying heed to the context in which she was dealing with the problem.

Kofi Annan report also concluded that "The international community should strive to fully understand the sensitivities that prevail in Rakhine State and work with the Government to achieve a positive vision for the future."[10]

Her full speech at the International Court of Justice is in the Appendix.

Aung San Suu Kyi stated that the government would take measures to address the problem, particularly to control the spread of hate. However, the international community denounced her for not taking a stronger stand and condemning the military. There were even calls for taking back her Nobel Prize. This only served to undermine Daw Aung San Suu Kyi's authority by undermining her international stature which strengthened the hands of the military junta, but did little to help the cause of the Rohingyas.

Aung San Suu Kyi is not an islamophobe and her legal advisor, Ko Ni, was a Muslim of Indian ethnicity. He was a former political prisoner and an outspoken critic of the military's involvement in politics as well as religious intolerance in his country. He was assassinated in January 2017.

In 2020, when the NLD led by Aung San Suu Kyi won the general elections and there was hope that the country could finally make a transition to democracy, the military staged another coup on 1 February 2021 and arrested the elected members of Parliament on the day they came together to take the oath. This time, Aung San Suu Kyi was arrested and sent to prison after false cases were foisted on her. She has even been denied medical treatment. There are some 20,600 political prisoners in prisons across the country, according to the Assistance Association for Political Prisoners.

The international community has not only been silent about Aung San Suu Kyi's arrest but has also largely ignored the brutal military rule, which has destroyed the country and sought to crush the spirit of its people by torture and executions.

Undeterred by the junta's ruthlessness, on 19 June 2023,

on Aung San Suu Kyi's birthday, women in Myanmar gathered across the country, symbolically carrying flowers as an act of resistance. Flowers are associated with the way Daw Aung San Suu Kyi wears flowers in her hair. Some women wore flowers in their hair, some carried a flower in the palm of their hand, shops sold flowers, and others posted photos on Facebook of themselves holding a flower in their hand.

In no time, the women were detained. According to the international media, the crackdown included anyone who dared to post a photo holding a flower or a birthday greeting. "How can the military be afraid of one person with a flower?" *The New York Times* quoted a man as saying.[11]

In 2024, the people went on a flower strike on their beloved leader's birthday. Images on social media showed protesters carrying Aung San Suu Kyi's picture and banners reading "Happy Birthday, Steel Rose" and "The steel roses will retaliate against the junta's oppression without yielding," referencing one of their hero's nicknames and adopting the sobriquet for themselves.[12]

In 2025, on Aung San Suu Kyi's 80th birthday, the Thailand-based Burmese news website, *The Irrawaddy* reported that the Indian Embassy in Yangon sent flowers to the NLD headquarters in Yangon's Bahan Township. As there was no one at the NLD office, the bouquet was reportedly left at the locked gate. A card with the flowers read: "Heartiest congratulations on the 80th birthday of Daw Aung San Suu Kyi. From the Embassy of India, Yangon."[13] Other embassies posted online birthday wishes.

In other parts of Myanmar, people displayed placards with Aung San Suu Kyi's famous slogan, "The only real prison is fear, and the only real freedom is freedom from fear."

However, after the coup of February 2021, Aung San Suu Kyi is no longer seen as the leader of the pro-democracy movement, even though her personal courage and moral strength continue to inspire the people. The new generation is looking for a more dynamic political party and younger leaders.

NOTES

1. I have used Burma if the reference is to the country before 1989 after which it is called Myanmar; the same for Rangoon and Yangon. Burmese do not have surnames or family names. As Aung San Suu Kyi says in her book, *Freedom from Fear* (1992), "It is not possible to tell from a person's name or accent whether his father is a manual labourer or a wealthy businessman." "U" meaning Uncle is used for older men who occupy an important position; the same way Daw which means Aunt is used for a woman occupying an important position. Ko is used for respect for men; it literally means older brother.

2. https://jacket2.org/commentary/train-comin-poems-burmese-resistance

3. Far an account of the hijacking see Nandita Haksar and Soe Myint, *Resisting Military Rule in Burma (1988-2024): Story of Mizzima Media—Born in Exile, Banned in Myanmar* (Aakar, 2025).

4. David Brenner https://thediplomat.com/2014/03/the-tatma daws-divide-and-rule-tactics-in-myanmar/

5. https://populationandsecurity.com/double-colonization-residential-schools-in-present-day-myanmar/

6. Pai Choimt Khaung and Haymarn Soe Nyunt in Visual Rebellion https://visualrebellion.org/timeline/echoes-of-the-   past-the-loss-of-the-jubilee-hall-and-the-students-union-build ings#:~:

7. https://www.newmandala.org/1974-u-thant-uprising-a-first-hand-account/ New Mandala is supported by the Australian" National University (ANU), a world-leading centre of research and teaching on Southeast Asia that has hosted the site since its founding in 2006.

8. John Charles Ryan, Verses of Resistance: Activist Poetry of Myanmar https://seamsa.org/wp-content/uploads/2020/10/07-article-2-22verses-of-resistance-the-activist-poetry-of-myanmar22-by-john-charles-ryan.pdf

9. Rachel Wong etc, Poetry and Politics in Myanmar, Interview on July 20, 2016 Point magazine https://thepointmag.com/politics/poetry-politics-myanmar/#:~:text=Maddy:%

10. https://www.kofiannanfoundation.org/wp-content/uploads/2017/08/FinalReport_Eng.pdf
11. On Aung San Suu Kyi's Birthday, Flowers, Then Arrests—*The New York Times.*
12. https://www.nbcnews.com/news/world/supporters-myanmars-jailed-leader-suu-kyi-mark-79th-birthday-flower-th-rcna157994
13. https://www.facebook.com/theirrawaddy/posts/indian-embassy-sends-birthday-flowersjune-20-2025the-indian-embassy-in-yangon-se/1156880633133759/

2

The Spring Revolution

Around the heart,
Planted like iron,
We need memories.

Without memories,
When the dead visit,
What shall we Offer?
　　　　　　　　　　　　　–Aung Khin Myint

The November 2020 elections filled the people in Myanmar with hope that their country would return to being a vibrant democracy. But there was also an ominous cloud of fear, because everyone knew that the military could stage a coup and cut short the transition to democracy. Perhaps it could best be described as hope without optimism.

Even though the people had some freedom to express themselves during the few years that National League for Democracy was in power the military did not allow anyone to cross the line.

Even a thangyat performance could land people in jail.

Thangyat is a popular traditional art form in Myanmar, which fuses poetry, comedy, and music, and is usually performed during Myanmar's New Year water festival in April. In 2019 the Peacock Generation staged a performance in which members of the group wore military uniforms and criticized the Myanmar military. The group livestreamed some of their performances on social media.

The members of the group were targeted and seven of the performers were arrested and detained and sentenced to anywhere between six months to one year in prison.[1]

In the lead-up to the November 2020 general elections, the military began planting seeds of doubt, knowing the National League for Democracy (NLD) was headed for another victory. After the elections in which the NLD decisively won, there was an increase in demonstrations by supporters of the military claiming election fraud. These demonstrations were often organised by the military-backed Union Solidarity and Development Party (USDP).[2]

Already, independent media houses such as *Mizzima* were finding secret hideouts for their journalists, knowing that the first target of any coup would be the media. They planned on moving to the relatively safe zones under the control of the ethnic armed groups; some political activists made plans to flee across the border to Thailand or India; and then there were the majority of the people who knew they would have to stay and confront the military.

On 1 February 2021, just a few hours before the new Parliament was to convene, Senior General Min Aung Hlaing, the commander-in-chief of the country's armed forces, staged a coup and declared a state of emergency by invoking Articles 417 and 418 of the 2008 Constitution on the grounds that the elections were won by fraud. All executive, legislative and judicial powers were appropriated by the commander-in-chief.

The International Commission of Jurists (ICJ) has said that by staging a coup, the military had violated Myanmar's constitution. The ICJ's General Secretary stated that the "Myanmar military's actions violated even the flawed Constitution that the military itself imposed in 2008."[3]

The junta wanted the coup to have legal legitimacy, and so they ordered the media to refer to the new government as the State Administrative Council (SAC) and not as the "regime" or the "junta". From the start, the independent media and the people had called it the junta. No one called the military rulers the Tatamadaw this time. They were referred to as the military, the force which was responsible for unprecedented cruelty.

The military detained State Counsellor, Aung San Suu Kyi, President Win Myint and other senior figures from the ruling NLD. This time, Aung San Suu Kyi was not placed under house arrest but put in prison. A handwritten note from Aung Suu Kyi was put on the NLD's Facebook page:

"I urge people not to accept this, to respond and wholeheartedly to protest against the coup by the military. Only the people are important."

The party said the note in Burmese was written in anticipation of a coup.

All 400 elected members of Parliament were detained, but later released. The 300 members of the NLD[4] met online and announced on Facebook that they had named a committee to carry out the functions of its parliamentary party. They also posted their letter to the United Nations, urging targeted sanctions and for businesses to cut ties with the military with its vast, lucrative holdings.

National Unity Government

On 5 February 2021, the NLD members and the elected officials from the 2020 general election, who were not arrested, managed to form a committee-in-exile called, "Committee Representing Pyidaungsu Hluttaw" (CRPH). The CRPH, many of whose members belonged to Gen Z, declared the military governing body, the SAC, a "terrorist group". On 31 March, it declared the military's 2008 Constitution abolished. Later, the CRPH was transformed into a government-in-exile, called the National Unity Government (NUG).

The NUG formed a cabinet in which the ministers were

from different ethnic nationalities, including Kachin, Karen, Ta'ang, Shan, Karenni, Kayan, Mon and Chin. This was the first time in the history of the country that the minority ethnic nationalities had found representation in the cabinet.

Significantly, the NUG appointed an openly gay minister, Aung Myo Min, a long-time activist in the LGBTQ movement, as Minister for Human Rights and a Rohingya, Aung Kyaw Moe, as his deputy.

In contrast to the government formed by Aung San Suu Kyi after the 2015 elections, when not a single woman was included in her cabinet (except for herself), the NUG has adopted the internationally-accepted Interim Gender Equality Policy (2024-26) in an effort to ensure gender-responsive governance. It has put women in charge of the education, health, and social welfare ministries. As per the Asian Network for Free Elections, under Suu Kyi's leadership, several other strategic positions that could and should have been filled by women, such as the Women's Affairs Committee, ironically had a majority of male committee members.[5]

This was for the first time in the history of Myanmar that such an inclusive government had been formed. This in itself was a significant milestone in the Spring Revolution.

Unprecedented Cruelty

From the start of the coup, it was clear that this time the military intended to rule with unprecedented brutality.

Those who had experience of the military crackdown of 1989-90 and had suffered detention under the military rulers said that this time the military was far more brutal. The UN Special Rapporteur on Human Rights in Myanmar, Tom Andrews, told the UN's Human Rights Council the country was "being controlled by a murderous, illegal regime."

Special Rapporteur Andrews informed the Council

that more than half of those killed were under age of 25. "There is extensive video evidence of security forces viciously beating protesters, medics, and bystanders. There is a video of soldiers and police systematically moving through neighbourhoods, destroying property, looting shops, arbitrarily arresting protesters and passers-by, and firing indiscriminately into people's homes," Andrews said.[6] He accused the regime of "engaging in crimes against humanity."

Ma Thida, a surgeon, author, and a former political prisoner who had taken part in the 1988 uprising and was jailed in 1993 for supporting the NLD, had this to say in an interview:

> "the military regime this time acting against its own people is like a terrorist organisation. The violence and the terror are very different. The way the military regime is practising is more terroristic; it's not just simple violent actions. So, the way it has handled the peaceful protesters is aiming at the protesters' heads to deliberately kill them, not just controlling them. They literally want to kill people, and they use over 100 airstrikes against the civilians. And they also use arson; they're burning villages and people alive as a weapon to crack down on the revolution. So, the way the military has been acting is more on the terror side right now.

> "...And another big difference is: In 1988, for the civilians, for the people, there was no legitimacy whatsoever. It was directly from the so-called socialist regime to the military takeover. But right now, in November 2020, there was a general election, and the elected members of parliament and the legitimacy is still vividly going on. But they try to undermine or they try to erase the result of the 2020 election. That's why, right now, for the civilian side, for the revolution side, they have full legitimacy. They have their own elected people to govern the country. There was a coup attempt. In '88, we can deliberately say there was a coup. Right now, it's just a coup attempt. They violated their own 2008 constitution."[7]

Incidents of extreme cruelty were reported from all parts of the country by both national and international media. There were incidents when the military threatened family members trying to bury their dead and, in several cases, seized their loved ones' dead bodies, demanding ransoms for their return.

The CNN reported, quoting a post on Facebook from the Bago University Students Union, that the military was now charging families 120,000 Myanmar kyat ($85) to retrieve the bodies of relatives who died in April 2021.[8] Many civilians have been maimed for life, losing limbs and eyesight. Myanmar Now reported that Hlyan Phyo Aung, a 22-year-old civil engineering student, was hospitalized after a soldier shot and destroyed his right hand at a rally in Magway on 27 March. After the hand was amputated, he was sent to Magway Prison, even though the doctors said he urgently needed eye surgery. His parents filed a bail application; his court hearing was postponed eight times.[9]

Every citizen of Myanmar has been touched by the junta cruelities, with more than 3.5 million people internally displaced without access to basic amenities such as safe drinking water or medical services. Since the 2021 military coup in Burma, UNHCR estimates that upwards of 55,000 people, mostly Chin refugees, have fled across the border to India. Of this number, at least 40,150 are in Mizoram state, which borders the Chin State. There are 8,250 Chin refugees in Manipur state, while 5,092 have presented themselves for registration with the UNHCR in New Delhi. But these numbers fluctuate.

There are approximately 80,000 refugees from Myanmar in nine temporary shelters managed by the Royal Thai Government (RTG) along the Thai-Myanmar border.

These numbers do not include the Rohingyas who were disenfranchised earlier and have fled to mostly Bangladesh but also to India, Malaysia and other countries.

These cold statistics do not convey the sufferings of the men, women and children who face not only a civil war and conflict within the armed groups, but also natural disasters such as the devastating earthquake of 7.7 magnitude which struck central Myanmar on 28 March 2025.

The litany of suffering could fill many volumes. But when you talk to the Burmese, they seldom speak of their suffering. They talk about their resistance, and about defeating the Myanmar military. Unlike the 1988 uprising, when the students spoke of abstract ideas of human rights and democracy, this generation is fighting much more for personal liberty. *New Oo Taw-Ihan Jay*, or the Spring Revolution, is as much about resisting the junta as it is about personal freedom for the youth who proudly call themselves Gen Z (born between 1997-2013).

The resistance to the military regime can be broadly divided into the armed resistance and the civil disobedience movement or the CDM.

Armed Resistance

For the first time in the history of Myanmar, the armies of the ethnic nationalities made alliances with each other and with the Bamar armed groups, called the Peoples Defence Force (PDF).

There were already some 25 active ethnic armies that have been fighting against military rule and for greater federalism for decades. These include the Kachin Independence Army (KIA), Shan State Army, and Karen National Liberation Army (KNLA).[10]

In 2023, these armed groups formed an alliance, posing the most serious challenge to the military regime since the coup of February 2021. According to media reports:

"In late October 2023, a coalition of three ethnic armed groups in Shan State launched a coordinated offensive—named Operation 1027, for the date the offensive commenced—

against the junta. Known as the Three Brotherhood Alliance, this coalition consists of the Arakan Army (AA), the Myanmar National Democratic Alliance Army (MNDAA), and the Ta'ang National Liberation Army (TNLA). Initially formed in 2019, the group's 2023 coordinated offensive posed the strongest challenge to military rule since the February 2021 coup. Insurgents used drones to bomb military and police outposts in eastern Kayah state, bordering Thailand; western Rakhine state, bordering India; and northern Shan state, bordering China."[11]

By 2024, almost 50 per cent of the territory of Myanmar had come under the control of the resistance forces.

In May 2021, the NUG formed its armed wing, called the People's Defence Force or the PDF, in which some 125 armed groups formed independently in different cities, towns and villages came together. Although these groups swore allegiance to the NUG, the latter did not always have control over their actions. Some in the PDF had alliances with ethnic armed groups who had decades of experience in armed resistance. Incidentally, Myanmar is home to the highest number of non-state armed groups.

In 2022, the PDF claimed 65,000 fighters, which, by 2024, had risen to 85,000 soldiers.[12]

These tough fighters, hardened by combat and living in dangerous conditions, find time to write poems, and their poems hit the target as accurately as their bullets.

Brig General Nyo Twan Awng, the Vice Commander-in-Chief of the Arakan Army and a trained doctor is one such poet. This Arakan doctor turned commander, who had attended the Panglong Conference organised by Aung San Suu Kyi in 2018, observed his 44th birthday by publishing a book of poems in March 2025 under his pen name, Thupone Phyu. The poems infused with defiance, humour and a touch of romance, reflect the spirit of the people involved in the most violent conflict in the world.

Here is a short poem called State Cup[13] of defiant optimism:

> Messi
> It's insignificant for us
> Whether you play in the 2026 World Cup
> Four years from now, or not
> You will certainly see
> Our State Cup Final match
> By the year 2026
> Including our matches
> If you haven't yet died

In another poem, entitled Rebel's Wife, he reminds readers that rebels, too, have families.

> Rebel has parents,
> Children and wife
> Rebel's wife can't be an ordinary woman
> To be a rebel's wife
> She must have a rebel attitude
> And she must be a rebel once
> Rebels are filled with full dedication
> And sacrifices
> To be a rebel's wife
> Please bring a sacrifice and a true vow
> Besides love
> Along with you
> I'm the brown rebel
> She's the white rebel

And then there are poems which reflect the rage that the people feel against the military regime, entitled State Administration Council (SAC):

> Min Aung Haling is the painter
> Adept in rough brush stroke
> Doing always strange things
> Really
> All touched with his brush strokes have become rebels

He made all who came from different backgrounds
To become the same personality
Made those who did not know the revolution
The revolutionaries
He is adept at remembering his name
In everybody's mind
So, he foresees Act V of his own play
Which will come soon

This year
The best things he can do are
Killing people
Burning houses
Girdling the future of youths
Being awarded the title of war criminal thrice
Rebel organiser for all ethnic people
Made all people become rebels[14]

*****

Maung Saungkha studied chemical engineering, and as a student, he founded the Poetry Lovers Club. Saungkha landed in prison for six months for a poem he wrote that allegedly spoke of a portrait of the former President, Thein Sein, tattooed on his penis. He denied the allegation and was not asked to prove it in court! The controversial poem:

On my manhood rests
A tattoo portrait
Of Mr President
My beloved found that out
After we wed
She was utterly devastated
Inconsolable.

This was in 2016 when Aung San Suu Kyi led the government. Maung Saungkha was put on trial. His case made international headlines. It was reported by the BBC and the *New York Times*, among others, in the western media, which was seeking to undermine Aung San Suu Kyi as an undemocratic ruler without giving the context to the challenges under which she was working.

A report from that time states, "Myanmar poet Maung Saungkha insists he does not have a portrait of his country's former President, Thein Sein, tattooed on his penis, although he was not asked to prove the point in court. But 24-year-old Mr Saungkha was still sentenced to six months in jail for defaming Mr Thein Sein in a case that highlights restrictions on free speech remain in Myanmar, where Nobel Peace Laureate Aung San Suu Kyi took power in April."[15]

On 17 April 2022, Saungkha became one of the founding members of the Burma People's Liberation Army (BPLA), one of the biggest PDF forces. The BPLA's objectives are the end of the Bamar Buddhist dominance over other ethnic groups and the establishment of a federal democratic government. Saungkha has warned that even if Aung San Suu Kyi is released, there should be no compromise with the vision of democratic federalism in the name of stability.

In an interview with *The Guardian*, Saungkha spoke of his difficult journey from a poet and human rights activist to a military commander:

> "During the three months of training, we ran drills and studied the battlefield and governance systems without rest from 4 am to 10 pm. To train our minds and bodies to become stronger, we were only allowed two meals a day, limited to five minutes, and we sometimes went days without eating. Outside food was also prohibited, and we were never able to fill our stomachs.

> "I have endured days under the scorching sun without a sip of water; I have also stood to attention under heavy rain to the sound of harsh commands that felt like hot liquid iron being poured into my ears, and have experienced the feeling that blows with a cane could fall on my hips at any time.

> "By the end of the training, my potbelly had disappeared

and I had turned to skin and bones. I used to get tired just climbing three floors of stairs in my city apartment building; now, I am running up and down hilly jungle terrain. My mindset had also hardened. I had lived my entire life as an anti-war poet. But the former peacemaker who once could not stand even the sound of gunfire is now hungry for war. I believe we have no other choice."[16]

Here is another poem by the Commander of the BPLA, written in December 2018, entitled Propaganda:

The story behind a pair of pants,
Unzipped.
Strands of dead hair
Jump off a photograph.
Fish in the papers are intellectually challenged.
Comings and goings for peace of mind and body,
a can of Coke shaken and opened,
the spill-over of truth from the outside world,
God knows, they say, but
The situation is that
what God knows isn't enough.
Only the dates at the top of the pages are credible.
A freight train loaded with post-truth heads for one town after another.

(Translated by Ko Ko Thett, a famous Burmese poet)[17]

For now, Maung Saungkha is training former chefs, ex-journalists, rappers and poets—people from all walks of life—to be soldiers with the clear objective of overthrowing the military regime that seized power in the coup of 2021.

Crowdfunding a War

During the 1988 uprising, western states and NGOs were enthusiastically funding the resistance, in contrast to the resistance since the coup of 2021, where support or humanitarian aid has been limited. As an activist of the Free Burma Campaign said, the United States (and that can be said for the west generally) backs resistance only if the backing advances "its core geopolitical interests."[18]

Besides, the west had trained its guns on Aung San Suu Kyi for not condemning the massacre of the Rohingyas more strongly. However, she was unable to outright condemn the Myanmar military when she was in government given that the army still held substantial power and the Rohingya massacre was backed by extremist Buddhists.

However, the lack of funding from the west has been made up by generous donations from the Burmese diaspora scattered all over the world, from the United States, Canada, to Norway, Sweden to Australia and New Zealand. These are people who were mostly refugees and were resettled through the UNHCR or private sponsorships after the crackdown in 1989, or even before that as in the case of the Rohingyas and ethnic minorities.

Perhaps the most remarkable fact is that the resistance is being crowdfunded. And this crowdfunding would not have been possible had it not been for the tech-savvy youth who knew how to manage digital transfers, avoiding legal hurdles.

It is worthwhile to quote from the report on crowdfunding with respect to Myanmar by the International Crisis Group:

> "Funding has been a central concern for Myanmar's junta and its opponents since the first days after the February 2021 coup d'état. Both sides have sought not only to raise money but also to deny it to their foes. The regime, with its control of the levers of state, has the advantage. But anti-military groups have held their own, adopting a variety of crowdfunding techniques, including innovative online methods, that have secured them enough resources to sustain a multi-faceted resistance movement. The amounts are far short of that required to threaten the junta's hold on power, but the regime has been unable to cut off the flow of funds. The conflict's trajectory now depends in part on whether

resistance forces can keep donations streaming in—and find more. They should seek expert advice on data security to ensure that people giving money are protected. ....

"Post-coup Myanmar is a vivid example of how conflict parties can weaponise the internet, a trend that is increasingly evident around the world. Against the odds, opposition forces have raised significant sums—possibly in the hundreds of millions of dollars—to help them fight the military regime. The mobilisation of funds, much of it in small individual donations from the diaspora, has been made possible by Myanmar's digital revolution and the democratisation of financial services over the past decade. This revolution created not only new means of raising and moving money, but also the knowledge people in Myanmar needed to take advantage of these tools.

"Widespread internet access has also been essential to efforts to weaken the military regime financially. Here, the results have been mixed. Some initiatives have been highly successful, such as the mass boycott by people in Myanmar of military-owned beer brands and their refusal to pay electricity bills. But others have had little impact or even been counterproductive, such as civil society groups pressuring the French energy conglomerate TotalEnergies to withdraw from the country. That campaign ended up providing the regime with more oil and gas revenue, since it was able to assume part of TotalEnergies' stake in a gas project for free.

"While Myanmar's anti-military forces have raised significant funds, like many decentralised insurgencies, they have found it difficult to move money to where it is needed. Even with its unsophisticated monitoring instruments, the regime has been able to push most opposition groups out of the formal banking system, sowing enough fear to make many in the country hesitate to donate to its adversaries. Anti-junta forces, particularly the National Unity Government (NUG), a parallel administration formed by opposition lawmakers, have also faced challenges using the international banking system, sometimes falling foul of regulations meant to police money laundering and terrorism financing. In response, the

NUG has begun using new technologies like cryptocurrency and blockchain, but these efforts remain embryonic; for the most part, anti-military groups have relied on informal remittances to skirt the regime's banking restrictions."[19]

Who are the diaspora that have managed to raise millions of dollars to fund armed resistance?

The report states:

"The diaspora is the single most important source of funding for Myanmar's resistance movement. It is large and dispersed; there are no precise figures, but millions of people of Myanmar origin live in Thailand, and hundreds of thousands more in both Malaysia and Singapore. Japan, Korea, the U.S., the United Kingdom, Europe, the Middle East and Australia also host sizeable communities. This diaspora is extremely diverse, made up of everyone from unregistered migrant workers and refugees to students and professionals, and it encompasses a wide range of ethnic and religious groups.

"Since the coup, individuals and (often pre-existing) community groups in the diaspora have raised millions of dollars. To reach potential donors outside their community, they have also held public events, such as exhibitions, movie screenings and other cultural activities, in their places of exile. While some of the funds raised are channelled to the NUG, they are just as often transferred directly to organisations (mainly resistance groups) or individuals on the ground.

"Some social media influencers abroad have also used their platforms to raise significant funds. Arguably the most prominent example is the U.S.-based Pencilo, whose Facebook posts direct her 1.6 million followers to various fundraising campaigns. In March and April, she reportedly helped raise more than $2 million for Project Dragonfly, which aimed to help resistance groups buy anti-aircraft weaponry.

"Activists have also developed new online platforms dedicated to raising funds for anti-junta activities. Click2Donate, for example, hosts content on various platforms and generates money from advertising. Since its launch in September 2021, its app has been downloaded more than 500,000 times, raising more than $1 million that has been distributed to hundreds of resistance groups. Another example is a mobile phone game, "War of Heroes", developed by a group of Myanmar coders and artists. They say they have raised almost $200,000 so far from the game's free and paid versions, all of which they have donated to resistance forces.

"More quietly, individuals and small networks abroad have also raised a significant amount of money. Although they can operate more openly than their counterparts in Myanmar, they often still shroud their activities in secrecy. Some of them live in countries that may be hostile to public fundraising for an armed struggle, while others are unable to reveal their identities because it could affect their careers, make it unsafe for them to return to Myanmar or put family members who remain in the country at risk. The chances of running afoul of global banking regulations designed to counter money laundering and terrorism financing are another reason to work under the radar."

Ban on Media and Social Media

Another feature of the resistance in the Spring Revolution in Myanmar is the role of social media both for mobilising support for the movement, raising funds, and also for the way the junta has used it for its own political purposes.

During the 8888 uprising, there was no social media and almost no access to the internet or mobile phones. But internet penetration has been growing rapidly in Myanmar, with the number of users increasing by 3.5 million between 2019 and 2021, bringing the total to 23.65 million internet users. More than half of the Burmese population actively used Facebook as of January 2021.

Immediately after the military seized power in the 2021 coup, Facebook banned the armed forces from its platform, citing the military's history of "exceptionally severe" human rights abuses and the clear risk of future military-initiated violence.

Facebook had previously admitted to playing a role in

the persecution of the Rohingyas. However, a month later, according to a study, Facebook violated its own policies.

According to one study, a month after Myanmar's military seized power, Facebook's own page recommendation algorithm was amplifying content that violated many of its own policies.

The study stated:

> "After Myanmar's military seized power in a coup on 1 February 2021, imprisoning the country's democratically elected leaders, Facebook banned the armed forces from its platform. The company cited the military's history of exceptionally severe human rights abuses and the clear risk of future military-initiated violence.

> "But a month later, as soldiers massacred hundreds of unarmed civilians in the streets, we found that Facebook's own page recommendation algorithm was amplifying content that violated many of its own policies on violence and misinformation.

> "In the lead up to the annual Armed Forces Day celebration on 27 March, the bloodiest day since the coup ..., Facebook was prompting users to view and "like" pages containing posts that incited and threatened violence, pushed misinformation that could lead to physical harm, praised the military and glorified its abuses.

> Offline that day, the military killed at least 100 people in 24 hours, including teenagers, with a source telling Reuters that soldiers were killing people "like birds or chickens."[20]

The military regime has banned both independent media and social media platforms. It not only bans them, but it has also been actively using social media, especially Telegram, to spread misinformation.

One study by Attila Mong for DW Akademie on the way the Myanmar junta has used social media noted:

> "By now, Telegram has become the most important platform for the military to disseminate its messages. From there,

they extend their reach across different platforms through their networks. They assert that Telegram is the only reliable space available for sharing information, and they actively encourage their ministries and other pro-military entities to make greater use of the platform.

"The military has established a wide network of accounts on Telegram, which work in a synchronised way to support its propaganda and counter the effects of independent media."[21]

According to Mong, individuals and entities loyal to the military, with followers between 50,000-100,000 subscribers, operate several channels on Telegram. This network of pro-military propaganda accounts not only spreads disinformation and harmful content but also launches counterattacks on independent media, labelling their content as "fake news." Besides, the military regime's social media platforms and state-controlled newspapers feature multiple accounts named "Fact Check", which focus on "fact-checking" information published by independent media outlets.[22]

The people were able to circumvent the ban on social media platforms by using VPNs. However, that too has been banned by the junta since 2024.

As a result the Myanmar junta is, according a study[23] "is cutting off millions of people from the world by banning the use of many Virtual Private Networks (VPNs)—the last remaining tool for accessing blocked social media apps, messaging platforms, and thousands of websites. In parts of Myanmar, people continue to suffer from one of the world's largest, most widespread, and pervasive internet shutdowns—already an enormous barrier to getting access to vital information or reporting serious human rights violations."

According to one study by Golda Benjamin and Wai Phyo Myint the internet traffic volume to many sites, including Facebook, has significantly dropped since the ban was imposed on 30 May, 2024. Using a VPN to access the internet securely and privately has become increasingly risky. Police have been doing random phone checks, arresting people under anti-terrorism laws if they catch them with Facebook or VPN apps on their phones.

Since the coup in 2021, the military has been building massive surveillance infrastructure. It has activated intercept technologies in its telecommunications infrastructure, installed a network of CCTVs all over the country, and enacted surveillance-enabling regulations on SIM and IMEI registration. With this recent VPN ban, people have lost secure communication channels and their ability to hide their online footprints.[24]

It is in this context that the significance of the independent media and the journalists working against all odds must be seen and appreciated. According to a 2023 report of the International Federation of Journalists, since the military coup on 1 February 2021, at least 176 journalists have been arrested, and four killed, with as many as 50 are still in jail or in police detention.

These statistics do not reveal the tragic story behind each of these journalists killed, tortured or detained. Even more importantly, the statistics do not reveal the unimaginable courage and dedication of the Burmese journalists working under extremely dangerous conditions without a thought to their safety.

****

On 8 March, 2021 the junta announced that it had revoked the licences of *Mizzima, Democratic Voice of Burma (DVB), Khit Thit Media, Myanmar Now* and *7 Day News* and ordered them to stop publishing and broadcasting immediately.

The stories of how Myanmar's independent media has managed to continue reporting and broadcasting under these very challenging circumstances deserve much more than a few paragraphs.

Mizzima Media, which has a presence across social media platforms, including its own television channel, did not stop broadcasting for a single day, despite the coup and the ban. They took shelter with the Karen National Union. *Mizzima's* struggle to survive is documented in a book published recently.[25]

The people living inside Myanmar have shown awe-inspiring courage in getting news out to the world. For instance, an anonymous photojournalist posted this on his blog soon after the coup:

"Working as a freelance Burmese photojournalist, I have been documenting Myanmar's Spring Revolution and the brutal crackdown by the military, doing so at great personal risk. Journalists have been pursued, more than 70 have been arrested, and some have been forced into exile. On the ground, we stopped wearing helmets marked "PRESS" when we realised soldiers were targeting photographers.

"Since February 1, I have been on the streets every day, photographing protests and clashes, and have encountered many challenges, working in the midst of gunfire (both live rounds and rubber bullets), teargas and stun grenades, and have had to flee military and police forces, hiding in random apartments with the help of civilians, and moving from place to place in the evening to avoid night-time searches and arrests.

"On the afternoon of March 31, as I got back to my car after photographing a group of peaceful protestors in downtown Yangon, two military vehicles attempted to arrest us; one of them rammed the car to stop me from leaving, and soldiers pointed their guns at me and the other reporters in the car. To my surprise, I managed to accelerate and get away before the soldiers had time to shoot.

"I am still in Myanmar continuing my reporting, and must therefore remain anonymous for obvious security reasons."[26]

The history of the 8888 uprising continues to inspire the protestors of the Spring Revolution. The Blue Shirt protest is one example.

Blue Shirt Protest

The Blue Shirt protest was so named after U Win Tin, journalist, democracy activist, founding member of the NLD, and one of Burma's most high-profile and respected political prisoners, refused to hand back his blue prison shirt on his release from prison in 2008 after 19 years of incarceration and vowed to wear a blue shirt every day until all political prisoners were released. "If there are no political prisoners.... I will take off my shirt, but up until now I haven't seen good indications," he declared.

People were urged to post a picture of themselves wearing blue on Facebook, Instagram or Twitter, etc, using the hashtag @ or #blueshirt4burma.

People shared photos on social media wearing blue shirts and holding up a hand with the name of an arrested person written on it.

U Win Tin epitomises the steadfastness of journalists in Myanmar to perform their duty despite the junta's brutal repression. He found various ways to write while in prison. He describes one of his methods in an interview:

> "As an alternative to paper for writing, I also used the plastic wrapping of our food parcels. I would get a nail from the roof beam, grind and sharpen it to a point, and then write on the plastic by scratching, or if the plastic wrapping was very thin, I would puncture the sheet with holes in the shape of letters. I would pass these on to other prisoners. But puncturing the plastic for messages was a laborious process. Sometimes it would take one or two days to write a message, especially since guards would be constantly walking around to check on us."[27]

Civil Disobedience Movement

After the military announced that they had taken over power, rumours spread like wildfire. One such rumour exhorted people to remain silent for 72 hours because the military was waiting for a riot to legitimise their coup.

Another story that made the rounds was that if people started protesting immediately, it would make it difficult for the international community to take up their cause. There were also rumours that Aung San Suu Kyi would be released.

As one of the students said, "During those early hours, we felt a sense of loss, were terrified by uncertainty, and filled with rage. We focused on spreading awareness through social media and seeking help from international figures whilst maintaining peace on the streets."

The civil disobedience movement started on the very first day of the coup with online protests.

Many people turned their social media pictures red to show their support for Aung San Suu Kyi or black to express their anger. But by the evening, people started banging metal utensils and blowing car horns in protest against the military; some lit candles on their balconies.

The civil disobedience movement, which began online, quickly came onto the streets of Yangon and Mandalay, and soon spread to all parts of the country.

While hundreds of thousands of people poured out onto the streets wearing red ribbons, the colour of the NLD flag, vendors decorated their shops with red balloons as a mark of protest.

From the very first day, the three-finger salute became a symbol of protest. The three-finger salute is a hand gesture made by raising the index, middle and ring fingers, while holding the thumb to the little finger, and raising the hand with the palm facing out in a salute.

The salute originated in *The Hunger Games* series and has been adopted by activists as a symbol of resistance in many pro-democracy movements across Southeast Asia, especially in Thailand, Hong Kong and Myanmar.

This is one of the most widespread symbols adopted from popular Western culture by the young activists.

In *The Hunger Games*, the three-finger salute symbolizes admiration and gratitude and is also a gesture of farewell to those who bravely go to battle an all-powerful tyrant. In Myanmar, the three-finger salute stands for freedom, equality and solidarity.

To get international media attention, protestors came up with innovative protest tactics; creating different themes, trolling the police, dressing up in eye-catching outfits, creating very bold protest signs which went from displaying deep messages to rather funny ones.

Online protestors across Southeast Asia have also come together to make a "Tea and Milk Alliance". This was a reference to the fact that in all the Southeast Asian countries, they have tea with milk, in contrast to China, where they drink dairy-free black tea. In April 2021, Twitter created an emoji in support of the Milk Tea Alliance, marking the first anniversary of this online formation.

Another way that people across Southeast Asia have cooperated is through online digital activism, such as an initiative called Rap Against Junta by MCs, producers, DJs, sound engineers, event organisers, and graffiti artists. The initiative released a song named *"Dictators must Die"* by Floke Rose and Cori Rey from Myanmar, in collaboration with artists from Indonesia, India, Taiwan, Thailand, and Hong Kong.

While the online protests are an important aspect of the Spring Revolution, it was, in fact, the trade unions that formed the organized backbone of those early protests.

Trade Unions

In 2011, as part of a wider reform process, trade unions were legalised in Myanmar after close to 50 years of being prohibited. With support, at times, from outside activists, hundreds of thousands of workers in the industrial zones around Yangon established workplace unions in just 10 years.

In Myanmar, there are two trade union federations, the All Burma Federation of Trade Unions (ABFTU) and the Federation of General Workers Myanmar (FGWM). The garment workers in 21 factories together made the FGWM in the Hlaingtharyar industrial zone, on the outskirts of Yangon, in September 2019. It was FGWM workers who led the anti-coup protests in Yangon and catalysed the Spring Revolution.[28]

The role of trade unions is seldom written about in the accounts of the Spring Revolution in Myanmar. In fact, it was the organized trade unions who were at the forefront of the protests.

Strikes paralyzed sections of the state bureaucracy, when three-quarters of Myanmar's civil servants struck work. Entire industries—such as private banking—have been shut down, and a growing number of state-run bank workers are now joining the strikes.

An estimated 60 per cent of state electricity workers also went on strike. Several power departments in Yangon, the country's largest city, said in Facebook posts that they are refusing to follow orders from the military to cut power during night-time raids. "Our duty is to give electricity, not to cut it", read one post.

State railway workers went on strike, refusing to transport soldiers to be used as strike-breakers. For an entire week, the rail networks in Yangon and Mandalay, in the centre of the country, were shut down. In response, riot police were deployed into the housing compounds of train drivers but were beaten back by crowds of angry students and workers.[29]

In one of the earliest mobilizations, medical workers from over 110 hospitals and health departments in 50 townships across Myanmar were among the first to go on strike, two days after the coup. In one government hospital, 38 out of 40 doctors and 50 out of 70 nurses struck work.

Instead of working under the government, they said they would be using mobile medical clinics, charity clinics and private hospitals to provide free medical services.

The Confederation of Trade Unions Myanmar (CTUM), the largest trade union federation in Myanmar, called for the first general strike on 8 February. Despite threats of arrest and growing repressive tactics from the government, workers in a wide range of sectors, including garbage collectors, firefighters, electricity workers, private bank employees, and garment workers, initiated waves of strikes, and many joined street demonstrations.

Seven teachers' unions, including the 100,000-strong Myanmar Teachers' Federation that covers primary and higher education and monastery schools, announced work stoppages. In response to the coup and threats to media freedom, members of the Myanmar Press Council and more than a dozen journalists at *The Myanmar Times* have resigned.

Employees from municipal governments and the ministries of Commerce, Electricity and Energy, Transport and Communications, Agriculture, Livestock, and Irrigation have joined strike actions, leaving many departments deserted. The labour actions hit the transportation sector particularly hard. Reports said 99 per cent of railway employees are on strike, leading to a shutdown of train services.

Striking workers managed to shut down the military-controlled Myanmar Oil and Gas Enterprise, Myanmar National Airlines, mines, construction sites, garment factories, and schools, creating economic costs for the military rulers. The workers were joined by consumers boycotting the military's extensive business interests in food and beverage products, cigarettes, the entertainment industry, internet services, banks, financial enterprises, hospitals, oil companies, wholesale markets and retail businesses.

In the forefront of the street demonstrations were the garment workers who had been agitating against the worsening working conditions when the government decided to open the country to foreign capital. A wave of militant strikes swept the garment sector in 2019 to demand higher wages and safer working conditions. The $6 billion industry, which employs 700,000 mostly female workers, supplies global brands such as H&M, Zara, C&A, among others. It accounted for 30 per cent of Myanmar's exports that year—up from 7 per cent in 2011, when the country's democratic reforms began.

With the military coup, the garment workers were among the first to call for street protests and mobilise in the street, knowing that they could be arrested and imprisoned. This helped boost the confidence of the civil disobedience movement. As Andrew Tillett-Saks, a labour organizer based in Myanmar, said, "The sight of industrial workers, largely young, women garment workers, seems to have deeply inspired the general public, broken down some of the fear, and catalysed the massive protests and general strike we are seeing now."[30]

Sagaing is home to several large copper mines operated by Chinese companies, including Sabetaung, Letpadaung and Kyisintaung. Around 7,000 Burmese workers are estimated to be employed at Kyisintaung and Letpadaung combined. Thousands of workers joined the strike, but some operations continued to run with the help of Chinese labour.

More than 2,000 miners from the Kyisintaung copper mines in Monywa District, a joint venture since 2010 between the military-owned Myanma Economic Holdings Public Co. Ltd. (MEHL) and Myanmar Yang Tse Copper Mining—a subsidiary of Beijing-based Wanbao Mining Limited—joined the civil disobedience movement against the coup.

The Letpadaung Taung copper mine in Sagaing's Salingyi Township, another joint venture between MEHL and Wanbao, also stopped operations after thousands of employees joined the movement by 8 February, 2021. Letpadaung has been estimated to be the biggest copper mine in Southeast Asia.

Many reports acknowledged that the 22 February general strike helped power a nationwide, non-violent civil disobedience movement in support of the NUG, the national government-in-exile.

The hundreds of thousands of migrant workers from Myanmar working abroad also organized significant demonstrations in various countries. In Thailand, a few dozen of the estimated three to four million migrant workers from Myanmar protested in front of the Myanmar embassy in the days immediately after the coup. In Japan, hundreds of Myanmar workers also held a protest outside the United Nations office, calling for the international community to action the UN-endorsed R2P doctrine and take on the responsibility to protect the people of Myanmar.[31]

R2P stipulates three pillars of responsibility:

Pillar One

Every state has the Responsibility to Protect its populations from four mass atrocity crimes: genocide, war crimes, crimes against humanity and ethnic cleansing.

Pillar Two

The wider international community has the responsibility to encourage and assist individual states in meeting that responsibility.

Pillar Three

If a state is manifestly failing to protect its populations, the international community must be prepared to take appropriate collective action, in a timely and decisive manner and in accordance with the UN Charter.

Women and the Spring Revolution

The first person killed in the course of the Spring Revolution was a young woman, Mya Thwe Thwe Khaing, who was injured two days before her 20th birthday when police tried to disperse protesters in Nay Pyi Taw in February 2021.

Burmese society is deeply traditional and patriarchal. This means that young women are most vulnerable to oppression at home and targets when they demonstrate on the streets. As of January 2023, 2,778 women have been arbitrarily detained, and at least 363 women have been killed (Radio Free Asia 2023).

The participation of a large number of women has changed the dynamic of the movement, with NUG committing itself to championing women's rights. The participation and protests of women aim at both protesting against military rule as well as patriarchy. The most prominent protest has been the Htamein Protest.[32] The Htamein protest with the slogan "Our Sarong, Our Flag, Our Victory" is a strong movement representing all women.

Young Burmese women broke the glass ceiling and left behind their traditional supportive image by positioning themselves at the forefront of the pro-democracy movement. Could the Spring Revolution give birth to a social, cultural, and gender revolution, which leads to the establishment of a more equitable society for women, from all ethnic and religious communities?

The Htamein Protest

One of the most famous creative acts of resistance led by young women was the Htamein (a sarong-like skirt worn by women) Campaign of 8 March 2021, International Women's Day.

Throughout the country, women hung their *htameins* (sarongs) on makeshift clotheslines above streets in cities and townships. From major cities like Yangon, Mandalay, and Naypyitaw, to towns in Kayin, Kayah, and Mon State, the *htamein* became a protective shield against the police and soldiers, who were too scared to walk underneath due to their superstitious beliefs.

There is a widespread superstition that women's undergarments are unclean and have the power to affect men's inner power (or glory). Tradition holds that King Anawrahta was gored to death after his *hpon* was affected by women draping their *htamein* over his effigy. The *hpon* under Theravada Buddhism refers to the spiritual power that only men possess.

It is widely believed that the *hpon* will diminish if men walk under or come into contact with menstrual blood, which by association includes women's undergarments and the *htamein*. Soldiers and senior military leaders are notoriously superstitious, and this protest went into challenging the heart of the patriarchal military institution.

Drawing on patriarchal gendered norms to mock and shame the senior generals, people stuck menstrual pads and women's underwear to photos of military Commander-in-Chief Min Aung Hlaing, even as images of these acts were widely shared online through social media platforms. Young men, in an act of solidarity, tied the *htamein* on their heads.

On International Women's Day the *htamein* was raised as a flag in a clear subversive act of defiance of the patriarchal institution and its superstitious soldiers. Led by young women primarily between the ages of 18 and 35, their slogan *"Nga Doh htamain, nga doh ah lan, nga doh aung bwe"* (Our Sarong, Our Flag, Our Victory) served as a direct challenge to the patriarchal social system and values underpinning conservative military-led authoritarianism.

In some respects, the use of the *htamein* in the Spring Revolution is symbolically connected to earlier efforts such as the 2007 "Panties for Peace" campaign to shame the generals. However, the female activists of Gen Z have been more assertive and have pushed gender boundaries much further than previous generations.

Songs, Poems and Music

Poets and Singers have always been an integral part of Burmese resistance to military rule. One example is the Kachin singer, Mun Awng. Despite strict censorship, Awng managed to produce one album a year in Myanmar, with his production team having used bribery to get his songs approved by officials.

While still in Myanmar in 1992, Mun Awng released an album recorded in a makeshift studio in the refugee camp where he lived. The album, called *Battle for Peace,* was released in Thailand and then smuggled into Myanmar on cassette tapes and played on Burmese-language radio stations broadcasting from abroad, as it was banned by the government.

When Awng went to Norway to work for the Democratic Voice of Burma radio, he took every opportunity to travel all over the world to sing Burmese protest songs to raise awareness on the condition of his people and fund-raise for refugees and for humanitarian assistance. In 2004, Mun Awng contributed to *For the Lady,* a compilation album created to raise funds for the US Campaign for Burma.

Mun Awng also performed a solo concert in support of the Spring Revolution and voiced his support for the armed resistance.

It is important to remember that even those who are part of the civil disobedience movement support armed resistance. Even Aung San Suu Kyi, who, inspired by Indian leaders such as Gandhi and Nehru, is committed to non-violence, has never condemned or criticised the armed struggle.

*****

In the very first days of the Spring Revolution, poets were killed, shot by snipers holding positions on top of a building and taking aim at them as they marched along with unarmed protestors.

K Zar Win (1982-2021) was one of the first poets to be killed. He was born to a peasant family in Latpadaung near Monywa in 1982. Latpadaung is the site of the copper mines owned jointly by the Chinese and the junta. For much of his young adult life, K Zar Win was a Buddhist monk, until he left the order, arguing that being recognised as a learned monk by the Myanmar military state was pointless.

In 2015, he marched with students along the 350-mile route from Mandalay to Yangon for education reforms until the rally was shut down near Yangon, and he, along with most of the student leaders, was arrested and jailed. He spent a year and one month in prison, after which he published his best-known work, a collection of long-form poems, *My Reply to Ramon.*[33]

In the 2020 election, he said he did not vote for the NLD, whose policies he was very critical of, but when the NLD won by a landslide and an election fraud was alleged as an excuse for the 2021 military coup, he was on the frontlines of the anti-coup protests. He was shot dead by Myanmar security forces at a protest in Monywa on 3 March 2021. Journalists reported seeing a video of two policemen dragging K Zar Win's corpse through the street, scraping the blood-stained asphalt, before throwing him into a van.[34]

One of his poems captures the military perfectly:

> They love their country
> Just the way they love to grate a coconut
> from inside out,
> for coconut milk.
> That's who they are.

*****

Pinky Htut Aung, a self-taught multi-instrumentalist and experimental artist, describes the first days of the civil disobedience movement in an article entitled Sonic Resistance.[35] She explains the significance of the banging of pots and utensils in Yangon in the early days of the coup:

> "In our tradition, banging pots and pans signifies the act of driving out evil. We would start hitting pots and pans at 8 pm every night. ...The nightly pot banging was followed by playing the song *Kabar Ma Myay Buu* (Until the End of the World). The sound of pots and pans after the curfew became the means to alert residents in the area that intruders were coming."

Kabar Ma Kyay Buu was the anthem for the 1988 protesters. Written by Naing Myanmar and adapted from US progressive rock band Kansas's 1997 classic *"Dust in the Wind"*, the song came back even stronger this time around, as it was sung and played through speakers every night.

Another song from the 1988 uprising was *"Thway Thitsar"* (Blood Oath) written by Htoo Eain Thin. She says the

> influence of this marching song is phenomenal. People don't seem to get bored of it and the lyrics and melody get stuck in your mind, the beat of the song sends your heart racing and your blood boiling. It united the people. The song is often looped and performed repeatedly, further increasing its energy and bringing people together.

The protestors needed songs to keep them motivated because they knew that it was going to be a long battle. One such song was *"Khun Arr Phyae Meenge"* (Don't give up little one) by singer-songwriter, Khin Maung Toe.

Some brought their snare drums to accompany the chants, which sounded especially effective when the protesters sang the *Thway Thitsar* song. The snare drum (or side drum) is a percussion instrument that produces a sharp staccato sound when the head is struck with a drum stick. Eain Thin said the sound of the snares empowered each protest chant, "accompanying our demands and the ultimate wish to end military rule. Having a rhythm always kept things flowing."

Celebrities would hold megaphones and lead chants, using their influence to attract larger crowds and to keep people motivated. This, in turn, put them at risk of being arrested.

Take the case of Benjamin Sum, a famous Chin singer, whose single *The Day We Meet Again* had garnered over a million views within 24 hours. That was in 2020, and Sum was on top of the world. He had finished as runner-up in the 2019 edition of the Myanmar Idol contest.

Music was his refuge after his sister died and his mother was diagnosed with cancer. His father had already died when he was barely a toddler. After the coup, Sum took part in anti-junta protests, making him a marked man and forcing him to flee to Mizoram, India after a three-day hazardous journey.

Some bands dared to have live performances in the streets, such as the GenerationZ MM group. With its revolutionary words and bass drum, it sounds like battle music—the type of songs that makes your hair stand on end. Despite the size of the band of up to 30 instrumentalists and a choir of about 20 members, the group managed to perform live in one or two places in Yangon. Their ten-minute performances gave an impetus to the protests. There were also a few pop-up performances in some neighbourhoods; very quick sets of just a few songs, often accompanied by poets expressing their rage, while people scouted the perimeter or barricaded the streets.

In contrast was the upbeat song, *"A lo Ma Shi"* (We don't Need), with its positive energy, that made protestors spontaneously clap along.

The *Mizzima* TV channel on YouTube would broadcast the revolutionary songs live, starting with *A lo Ma Shi* at

8 pm, perfect for those who protested with pots and pans indoors. Pinky Htut Aung remembers singing and dancing to the song, while rhythmically hitting a metal plate.

In addition to the sonic resistance, Aung describes the 100 Projects campaign, in which people use projectors to display 10-minute video compilations of artworks, illustrations, photographs, and video clips in support of the Spring Revolution. The videos are screened indoors and outdoors on buildings, landmarks, and public spaces. The nationwide campaign now also includes participants from other countries who are against Myanmar's military rule.

Interestingly, this generation of protestors does not believe in any leader or party and is critical of even the NUG. "To...Ma Ma Nu Gyi," an elegiac anti-war poem, has highlighted the divide among opponents of military rule. Myanmar-based independent analyst Naw Theresa, writing for *The Diplomat*, described the controversy the poem caused among the resistance because it was critical of the National Unity Government.[36]

Written and published on his Facebook page by Maung Saungkham, the popular pro-resistance poet, the 400-line, 25-stanza poem is infused with anti-war sentiment. It takes little imagination to figure that *To.. Ma Ma Nu Gyi* is referring to the opposition NUG.

The narrator argues that war is easy when waged with words, but brutal when fought with human lives. Saungkham invokes cannibalism to describe civil war, saying that it is akin to using bits of fish to lure more fish or cutting off a mouse's tail to use as bait in a mouse trap.

From its introduction and up to the seventh stanza, the narrator sets the scene of a bus ride into Anyar region (the Day Zone consisting of central upper Myanmar) in the hope of finding the titular Ma Ma Nu Gyi. The poem references the aerial bombing, the burning of villages, extortion at checkpoints and hurried stops to piss as in prison vans.

From the eighth to the 15th stanzas, the poem goes into vivid descriptions of the devastation of the villages and how the military repeatedly abuses the country and its people with impunity.

The poem provides evocative snapshots of how the Dry Zone has become a living hell: homes built with frugal savings and remittances now burnt down or abandoned; a farmer wailing as he hugs his dead ox and asks how he will manage to plant his next crop; an elderly woman crying about how "they" (i.e. regime troops) cooked her chicken with the very fire they used to torch her home; and another finding solace in the fact that her Buddhist altar was left unscathed while the rest of her home burned down.

From the 16th stanza, the poem is critical of the NUG.

The poem was attacked for criticizing the NUG in the midst of the civil war, forcing the poet to delete it from his Facebook page which had half a million followers. However, many netizens had already copied the poem and shared it; it was even used by the junta for their own propaganda. Other critics pointed out that the poem suited the fancy of "non-violent activists, moderate revolutionaries and foreign governments seeking conflict de-escalation and political solutions to the civil war, [and] regime apologists and lobbyists."

The fact is that the NUG has a very difficult task before it of governing in the midst of a bitter and violent war; it also has to forge a unified vision for a future for Myanmar that brings together all the warring groups.

Artists too have come together to contribute to the civil disobedience movement. They quickly established an Association of Myanmar Contemporary Artists (AMCA) They set up what they call an Artist Street in front of the High Court in downtown Yangon, where they are painting in situ and selling artwork to support the civil servants who have stopped going to work in support of the CDM.[37]

A unique feature of the current resistance—and perhaps a challenge to a unified future—has been its strong emphasis on individual courage and individual freedom as reflected in the Freedom Tattoo Campaign which celebrates the courage of the protestors and the value they have put on individual liberty.

Tattoos as Resistance

The most distinctive art form in the Spring Revolution is the use of tattoo as resistance.

Burma has a long history of tattoos, but it is during the Spring Revolution that tattoos are being used as a form of resistance. Tattoo artists gave free tattoos of the symbols of the Spring Revolution; they tattooed the words "Spring Revolution", "Freedom from Fear" (the famous words of Aung San Suu Kyi) and drew portraits of the NLD leader in all sizes, from small ones on the arms to full portraits on the back.

The Freedom Tattoo Campaign began to commemorate the death of a famous Burmese kickboxer, Too Too, who died in prison. *Mizzima* carried a story[38] on the campaign, quoting Esther, one of its leaders, who explained that while the tattoo is painful, it will remain on the body for a lifetime, reminding us of the pain of the dictatorship. The campaign, according to the report, ran from 30 October to 3 December 2021, and is planned to continue in the rest of the country.

Pottu, a tattoo scholar involved in the campaign, says that the images of the Aung San Suu Kyi, the Spring Revolution and the three-finger salute tattoos are the best way to make fun of the military junta. Kyaw Htoo Bala, a 28-year-old art school graduate, created quite a stir by inviting dozens of artists to contribute their version of the salute, breaking with the habit of self-censorship.

Tattoo is a way of expressing a commitment to the cause, an abiding reminder of the goals of the Spring Revolution.

From big cities like Yangon and Mandalay, to Shan state's Nyaung Shwe, a small town near the popular tourist spot of Inle Lake, protesters are getting inked for democracy.

In one instance, eight tattooists inked dozens of participants who were each asked for a minimum donation of $2. Each tattoo took about 20 minutes to complete and, for speed, participants were given a choice of four styles: the face of Aung San Suu Kyi, the words "Spring revolution," the phrase *"Kabar Ma Kyay Bu"* (from the protest song) and the ubiquitous "three-finger salute," from *"The Hunger Games"* series.

The most popular design? An outline of Suu Kyi's face.

Aung San Suu Kyi's younger son, Kim Aris, has taken the Freedom Tattoo Campaign forward by having both his arms tattooed with the image of the mythical naga snake as part of a campaign for humanitarian aid to help millions displaced by the 2021 military coup.

Launched in October 2023, the campaign has successfully raised over 100,000 pounds (more than $125,000) to support victims of the "forgotten conflict" in Myanmar.

Aris told the Spanish news agency, EFE , in an interview that the campaign used the mythical snake as a tribute to the renowned kick-boxing fighter Too Too, who likely died under torture in a military prison in 2021.

This generation has exhibited exceptional courage and has shown its capacity to fight on the streets. They have also found unique ways to express themselves in their poems, songs, and tattoos.

A Burmese journalist Saw Kapi has written that there has been a paradigm shift in Myanmar's politics and that is why the people's revolution continues to make progress on the ground without any significant support from the international community.

Saw Kapi writes: "The Spring Revolution is more

than a political movement that aims for regime change. What is taking place in Myanmar today is a kind of *revolution of thought*—a revolution of how we think about and understand ourselves, our country, our histories, our cultures, and our future, compelling us to unwrap old lies and propaganda and achieve our collective potential as a country and union of peoples."[39]

NOTES

1. https://www.amnesty.be/IMG/pdf/i_will_not_surrender.pdf
2. Myanmar's Spring Revolution, July 2021 https://acleddata.com/report/myanmars-spring-revolution
3. https://www.icj.org/myanmar-military-coup-detat-violates-principles-of-rule-of-law-international-law-and-myanmars-constitution/
4. Besides the National League for Democracy and the Military backed USDP there were many ethnic based political parties who had put up candidates and won such as the Shan nationalities Party, Arakan Party, Chin National League for Democracy etc
5. https://thediplomat.com/2019/08/dashed-hopes-for-myanmars-women/
6. https://www.aljazeera.com/news/2023/2/1/timeline-two-years-since-the-myanmar-military-coup
7. Episode #54: 900 Days of the Spring Revolution. Mit Ma Thida https://www.ifa.de/en/podcast/myanmar-900-days-of-the-spring-revolution-with-ma-thida/
8. April 12, 2021 report https://edition.cnn.com/2021/04/11/asia/myanmar-families-bago-bodies-intl-hnk/index.html
9. July 1, 2021 Myanmar Now https://myanmar-now.org/en/news/student-protester-maimed-in-attack-by-soldiers-left-out-of-prisoner-release/
10. Antonio Graceffo, Backgrounder: Ethnic Armies in Myanmar Civil War, February 27, 2024, https://www.geopoliticalmonitor.com/backgrounder-ethnic-armies-in-the-myanmar-civil-war/
11. https://www.cfr.org/global-conflict-tracker/conflict/rohingya-crisis-myanmar
12. ibid
13. Poems translated by Ko Nyo Htun working in *Mizzima*
14. Translated by Soe Myint
15. https://www.smh.com.au/world/penis-poet-maung-

saungkha-sentenced-to-jail-for-defamation-then-released-20160525-gp368h.html
16. https://www.theguardian.com/global-development/2022/feb/09/hungry-for-war-my-journey-from-peaceful-poet-to-revolutionary-soldier-myanmar
17. https://maungsaungkha.wordpress.com/2018/12/02/propaganda/
18. https://www.aa.com.tr/en/analysis/opinion-6-reasons-us-is-not-really-supporting-myanmar-s-democratic-resistance/2699374
19. Crowdfunding a War: The Money behind Myanmar's Resistance International Crisis Group Report, December 2022.
20. https://globalwitness.org/en/campaigns/digital-threats/algorithm-of-harm-facebook-amplified-myanmar-military-propaganda-following-coup/
21. Attila Mong, Myanamr's military weaponizes disinformation https://akademie.dw.com/en/how-myanmars-military-regime-weaponizes-disinformation-against-independent-media/a-68672257
22. https://globalwitness.org/en/campaigns/digital-threats/algorithm-of-harm-facebook-amplified-myanmar-military-propaganda-following-coup/
23. Worse than China or Iran? Myanmar's dangerous VPN ban—Access Now
24. https://www.accessnow.org/myanmar-vpn-ban/
25. See: Nandita Haksar and Soe Myint, *Resisting Military Rule in Burma (1988-2024): Story of Mizzima Media—Born in Exile, banned in Myanmar* (2025).
26. https://www.visapourlimage.com/en/festival/exhibitions/la-revolution-du-printemps-en-birmanie
27. https://www.guernicamag.com/the-tiger/
28. Ko Maung, Myanmar's Spring Revolution: A History from Below Open Democracy, December 15, 2021https://www.opendemocracy.net/en/beyond-trafficking-and-slavery/myanmars-spring-revolution-a-history-from-below/
29. Robert Narai, Myanmar's Spring Revolution February 2021 https://redflag.org.au/article/myanmars-spring-revolution
30. Kevin Lin in Labor Notes https://labornotes.org/2021/02/myanmar-workers-and-unions-front-lines-fight-against-coup
31. https://www.un.org/en/genocide-prevention/responsibility-protect/about

32. The Role of Young Women in Myanmar's Spring Revolution https://muse.jhu.edu/pub/5/article/889923 Written by Marlar, Elena and Justina Chambers

33. https://adimagazine.com/article_author/k-za-win/

34. https://www.europeanpressprize.com/article/the-poets-army/

35. https://www.goethe.de/prj/nus/en/mag/hsw.html

36. I have taken the description of the poem from Naw Theresa's article published in the Diplomat How a Poem Briefly Shook Myanmar's Resistance Movement https://thediplomat.com/2024/07/how-a-poem-briefly-shook-myanmars-resistance-movement/

37. https://www.frieze.com/article/artists-protest-myanmar-coup-2021

38. The story was in Burmese and translated by *Mizzima* for this book

39. https://thediplomat.com/2022/07/understanding-myanmars-spring-revolution/

Funeral of Poet K Zar Win, killed by the military on March 3, 2021. His body is being taken to his village.

Htamein Protest: Our Sarong, Our Flag, Our Victory in 2021

Photos: Aung Nay Myo

Mass protests against the military coup of February 2021 in Monywa

Aung Nay Myo, the photo journalist covering the 2015 elections when Aung San Suu Kyi and her party, NLD, won with an overwhelming majority

Above, details of the tattoo on Aung Nay Myo with images of people executed or killed by the Myanmar army. Below, tattoo of the two friends Wai Moe Naing, student leader from Monywa in jail, and Aung Nay Myo, a refugee in India

Two Friends: Wai Moe Naing and Aung Nay Myo during the
protests against the coup before his crackdown

Protests against the military coup of 2021 ir Monywa with
Buddhists supporting the Civil Disobedience Movement

3

Aung Nay Myo: Portrait of An Activist

missing mother terribly
I remember home
Wanting to return to my village
But I can't
Where now I live
Neither my country nor my village
    —Tee Noe Karen, Resentful Refugee Life[1]

What does it mean to live under military rule, and how does one cope with the deaths, devastation, the loss and the grief? Pro-democracy activist Aung Nay Myo describes how he became active in the protests from the early days of the 1990s and is still active today. He forms a bridge between the early activists and the present generation.

Although his story is uniquely his, the experiences he has had and the situations he has faced are similar to the hundreds of thousands of citizens of Myanmar living under military rule for decades. They have pinned their hope on their Spring Revolution.

Aung Nay Myo had to flee his country and take shelter in India. Living in exile, adjusting to the life of a refugee, thinking of home and of his friends and comrades who have been executed and those who are living in jails under unbearable conditions he decided to have their faces tattooed on his back.

It was his way of expressing anger against military

rule—the bottom of his tattoo says: "Fuck Military Rule 1.2.2021". It is also his way of expressing his love for those who have given up their lives for the country. He says he will continue to get tattoos of others as the Spring Revolution continues....

This is his story, in his words (translated from Burmeses):

I was born in 1978, ten years before the national uprising against military rule in 1988.

I saw a glimpse of democracy from 2015 to 2020, but in 2021, the military carried out a coup, and my country was once again under military rule, this time much more brutal than we had ever experienced.

Throughout my life, I have been resisting military rule, and this is one fact which has defined my life, the choices I have made, and the times I have gone to jail, and that I am now a refugee in India facing the threat of deportation.

This is my story. But my story is no different from the stories of my people. In fact, I am one of the lucky ones who is not in jail like my friends, and am alive to speak and continue to resist.

I was born in Monywa, the capital city of Sagaing Region, Myanmar, about 136 kilometres north-west of Mandalay on the eastern bank of the River Chindwin. The Sagaing Region borders the Chin State and India's North-eastern states of Nagaland, Manipur and Arunachal Pradesh.

Monywa is famous for its Buddhist temples, including the colossal statue of Buddha, which is 381 feet tall and was completed in 2008. But there are much older Buddhist temples from the 10th to 15th centuries, such as the Thanboddhay Pagoda. It is part of a mammoth complex consisting of over 500,000 Buddhist images.

One of the most famous spiritual teachers from this region was the Venerable Ledi Sayadaw (1846-1923), who was known for inscribing scriptures in stone and reviving the ancient meditation practice of Vipassana.

Sayadaw founded a forest monastery in the "Ledi forest". It was from this monastery that he would take his name, Ledi Sayadaw, meaning "respected teacher of the Ledi forest."

In 1885, Ledi Sayadaw wrote the *Nwa-myitta-sa,* a poetic prose letter that argued that Burmese Buddhists should not kill cattle and eat beef, since Burmese farmers depended on them as beasts of burden to maintain their livelihoods, that the marketing of beef for human consumption threatened the extinction of the buffalo and cattle and that the practice was ecologically unsound. He subsequently led successful beef boycotts during the colonial era, despite the prevalence of beef eating among locals. He influenced a generation of Burmese nationalists in adopting this stance.

Our family was also influenced by his teachings and abstained from eating beef. Although I was brought up as a Theravada Buddhist, I do not practice my religion in the old ways of my ancestors.

Childhood

I was born in a typical Buddhist Burman family with nine siblings; I am the fifth from the top. My eldest brother was six years older than me.

Our house was in downtown Monywa, so even as a child I witnessed long processions of people shouting slogans and carrying the flags of the National League for Democracy (NLD) under the leadership of Daw Aung San Suu Kyi; I even had a glimpse of her at one of the rallies in 1988-89; and again in Tepayan in 2003, the year of the massacre of the NLD cadres. But I will come to that later.

My father's name is U Bo Gyi, and my mother's name is Daw Khin Sint. The Burmans do not have surnames or family names. It is not possible to tell the social origins of a person from the name.

My father was a trader and later opened a restaurant

in 2007, which was run by all of us. My parents consulted an astrologer who suggested the name "Soe" for their restaurant.

My mother was a busy housewife coping with her nine children. I never really got to live with her. I had hoped that once the Revolution is over, I would spend time with her but she passed away in September 2024, when I was living as a refugee in India.

My upbringing was strict, and all of us siblings had tasks assigned to us. In the mornings, we had to look after the shrine of Lord Buddha, clean the place, water the plants and put fresh flowers and offer alms to the monks who came around.

From the time I was a little boy, I used to see a black and white photo of General Aung San (1915-48) along with an old sepia photo of my grandfather, U Kyar, hanging in our sitting room. That is the only image I have of him because he had passed long before I was born.

My father was never tired of telling us how his father (my grandfather) was given a gallantry award by General Aung San himself during the anti-colonial movement. Like everyone else, we called the General by his honorific name, Bogyoke Aung San. My grandfather had been a member of the Anti-Fascist People's Freedom League (AFPFL), which was a broad popular front that ruled Burma between 1947 and 1958.

I had only heard some stories about my grandfather because he had died long before I was born. Gen Aung San was the father of Daw Aung San Suu Kyi. She had married an Englishman and lived in England along with her two sons. She had come back to Burma to nurse her mother in 1988, which is how she became involved in the national politics.

I had also read about Gen Aung San in school—we learnt a song in praise of Gen Aung San, the lines of which

I still remember. There was even a poem about how he had tried to bring all the ethnic nationalities together at the famous Panglong Conference in February 1947. Gen Aung San was unfortunately assassinated, but the question of ethnic nationalities continues to be central to our pro-democracy movement.

I studied in State High School No. 1 in Monywa.

My first memory of resistance to army rule is in 1991, when I was in grade four, and I noticed the older students had put up the NLD flag with a fighting peacock on a bamboo pole in our school. I had also carried a small flag in my schoolbag, and we took out a procession within the school compound and shouted slogans.

It was during one such procession in our school when the riot police came into the premises and beat up the students. I was injured on the forehead; I was bleeding. The senior students took me to hospital. It was that experience that created within me a deep hatred of the Burmese military.

The children of army officers came to our school in a special bus. There were some of these children in my class. They did not mingle with the other students. There was the daughter of a Tactical Commander, who would even beat up a student she did not like, but we could not touch her. I also knew there were special stores where all kinds of goods were available for decent prices, that only the army officers and their families had access to.

I heard slogans against Gen Ne Win, who was called a dictator and a fascist, but I was too young to fully understand the history of the regime.

I had one teacher, Myint Aung, who would give me some of the political pamphlets that were secretly circulating at the time. We did not have access to any Xerox machines, so we would copy them by hand. The Student Union also brought out a magazine called *Owei*, which means the cry of a fighting peacock.

My father discouraged me from taking an interest in politics and told me to focus on my studies. Even if I put on a tape of revolutionary songs, he would turn the tape off in case the police or army heard the songs, many of which were banned.

In 1993, when I was in seventh grade, a friend gave me a cassette of Mun Awwng, (b. 1960) the stage name of a famous Kachin singer, songwriter, and pro-democracy activist. His music, a mixture of Western rock and Southeast Asian ballads, was an integral part of the student protests in 1988, 1996 and 2007.

The album my friend gave me was called Tempest of Blood. My friend had smuggled it from Tamu, on the India-Myanmar border.

When I put on the cassette, my father immediately turned it off.

The album included the famous song *Kabar Ma Kyay Bu* (a spin on *"kaba ma kyay"*, which is the Burmese national anthem). *Kabar Ma Kyay Bu* was written and first sung by the famous songwriter and singer Naing Myanmar (1958-2025) The melody was copied from *'Dust in the Wind'* by the American group, Kansas. Naing Myanmar sang this song during the 1988 uprising.

The song is still sung in anti-coup protests today. It was a dangerous song to sing as it spoke of "democracy" and mentioned the name of Aung San Suu Kyi's father. It amounted to defiance of the authority of the junta. In Myanmar, under military rule, playing revolutionary songs can invite arrests, torture and long years of detention.

Below is the English translation of the song:[2]

> There is no pardon for you till the end of the world
> Cause that's the bloody record written by the people's lives
> The Strong Revolution!
> Oh the brave Heroes died for Democracy
> Our country, Myanmar, is a place built with Martyrs

And with strong affirmation and lack of fear to fight against
the Monsters,
Our people.
Dear Grandpa Kodaw Hmaing*, who fought against Colonies
with a pen
Our history was shamefully destroyed by our Myanmar
military itself
Oh our leader Thakin Aung San, who tried to get
independence, please look at us from heaven—our country is
bloody now
What the hell! No mercy, just bullies
Dead bodies are every where
Helplessly lying on the road
Hey! My brothers, my sisters and friends
That bloodbath can still be felt
And so, don't confuse it
As the fallen Heroes
Let's bravely fight for our democracy
Cause we are the one who unconditionally love our country
We swear, we will never forgive what you have done.

This song is sung by the famous singer Mun Awung
whose real name is Denis Daws. He had to flee the country
during the 1988 uprising because of state repression, but
even while in a refugee camp, he continued to write his
songs. He finally made his way to Norway to work at the
Democratic Voice of Burma, a radio station working for the
pro-democracy movement.

The other singer I liked is Lay Phyu, who was from Shan
state. He would come to Monywa to stay with his friend
Kyaw Aung Thit (popularly known as KAT), who wrote
many of the lyrics of his songs. I would go often to the
bookshop run by Kyaw Aung Thit. He moved to Yangon
and died in 2013. Many famous musicians and singers, as
well as the rock band Iron Cross, were there to mourn his
passing.

---

* Thakin Kodaw Hmaing (1876-1964) was a poet and witness to
  Burmese King being sent to India in exile.

Fighting Peacock

In 1996, all colleges and universities were shut down by the military because of widespread protests by students all over the country. In Monywa, the schools were still running and I was able to pass the metric exams in 1997, but could not continue my studies. It was only in 2001, when colleges and universities reopened, that I was able to pursue my college degree.

It was during this time, when all educational institutions were closed down, that my cousin brother returned to Monywa from Yangon where he was studying at the Yangon Institute of Technology (RIT). That was the institute where the students' protests had started before the 1988 uprising.

My cousin brought pamphlets and told me about the student activities in Yangon. He gave me a pamphlet which explained the difference between the symbol of the Fighting Peacock used by the students' movement and the image of the fighting peacock in the flag of the NLD.

Incidentally, the dancing peacock was used as the symbol of the Burmese monarch. During the period of the Konbaung Dynasty (1752-1885), the national flag had a dancing peacock on a red sun. It was also stamped on the highest-denomination coins minted by the Konbaung dynasty. Because of this association with the Konbaung monarchy, the anti-colonial nationalist movements widely used it. Upon independence, it was again featured on Burmese banknotes from 1948-66.

The Burmese student movement changed the symbol to a golden fighting peacock during the 1920s. And in 1988, when the NLD was established, they made the Fighting Peacock their symbol on their flag. They had adopted it from the students' movement.

But my cousin pointed out to me that the Fighting Peacock in the NLD flag has its feet together, whereas the

Fighting Peacock image of the Burmese students' movement has a circle around the peacock with one leg outside the circle, symbolising defiance.

When I was in school, the NLD office seldom organised any activities. They celebrated Gen Aung San's birthday. On some special occasions, they distributed free food to children. In those days, the repression was too severe for any open political activities. All the time that Daw Aung San Suu Kyi was under house arrest, the members of the NLD Party in Monywa did not dare to carry out any protests.

I was fascinated by the symbol of the Fighting Peacock of the students' movement, and I kept practising drawing the symbol till I could make it perfectly. This was a skill that came in handy in 1996 when there was another student uprising, and we needed a flag. When we went to the NLD office to ask for a flag, they shooed us away.

We then went to the Masoyien monastery, in Mandalay and asked the monks to give us a robe; I painted the fighting peacock on a monk's robe. But we were unable to use it because of a crackdown on the students. This was 1996, when the students' protests had reached their climax.

1996 Student Uprising

Amnesty International brought out a report on the events leading to the widespread student protests in 1996. I quote the report because I was in Monywa and still a school-going child. I only heard of the momentous events from my cousin and his friends, who had returned from Yangon after all educational institutions had closed down.

Between 1991 to 1996, there was little political activity, but by the end of 1996, student activism had become widespread; it spread from Yangon to other towns and cities across the country.

These protests were in the background of the political tensions between the ruling State Law and Order

Restoration Council (SLORC),[3] Myanmar's military government and the NLD, the primary legal opposition party. The military took pre-emptive steps, including mass arrests of NLD supporters by the security forces to prevent meetings, sentencing of dozens of NLD members to long terms in prison, restrictions on movement, and intensified surveillance and intimidation of NLD members and leaders.[4]

Early on 28 September 1996, security forces even blocked access to the street in front of Daw Aung San Suu Kyi's compound, where weekend public meetings had been convened for over one year.

This the time when Myanmar introduced email service and computers although most of us had not seen a computer or knew how to send an email. A 2011 report of the USA-based Freedom House reports on the restrictions on use of computers:

> The government's first attempt to restrict internet freedom was the 1996 Myanmar Computer Science Development Law, which made possession of an unregistered computer modem and connection to unauthorized computer networks punishable by up to 15 years in prison. Other laws and actions since then have furthered the government's efforts to clamp down on unsupervised internet use. Internet access and usage are extremely limited due to government restrictions, lack of infrastructure, and widespread poverty. The number of internet users is difficult to ascertain, as independent surveys are not available, and the government offers little credible reporting on these statistics. According to the International Telecommunication Union, there were 110,000 internet users as of 2009, amounting to 0.2 per cent of the population. MPT reports that there are 400,000 internet users in Burma. The price of a private internet connection is prohibitively expensive in a country where an estimated 32 percent of the population lives below the poverty line...

As I said I had not seen a computer, nor had I or my fellow students ever used one. We were still cyclostyling our leaflets, and we did not have access to mobile phones or laptops, although we had heard of these things. Even our electricity supply was not regular.

In the last three months of 1996, Burmese students staged large-scale demonstrations for the first time since 1991, when demonstrations in December that year had called for the release of Daw Aung San Suu Kyi and celebrated the 1991 Nobel Peace Prize awarded to her.

Initial protests revolved around the alleged beatings during the detention of three Burmese students by municipal police in October, but the student demands later grew to calls for the establishment of a student union and more academic freedom.

My cousin said the students were demanding the right to have student unions because, since 1962, the student unions had to function secretly, and this made them vulnerable to arrests. The students also wanted the restoration of the Senate Committee of Rangoon University, which had been banned when the military took full control over both the curriculum and the appointment of teachers.

Student Protests in Monywa

After listening to stories of student protests in Yangon from my cousin and other students who had come back to Monywa after their colleges had been closed down, my friends and I also wanted to do something in our hometown.

We sat at a teashop on Kyawkkar Road in a suburb of Monywa to plan how we could protest and what actions we could take. We thought we could begin by writing our own leaflet. We were having an animated discussion when we noticed that someone was watching us. It was difficult to find a safe place to discuss these things, so we decided to go to a cemetery. The cemetery was called Nayung Pin Shay, or the Big and Tall Banyan Tree.

We did not dare go on motorcycles because they made

too much noise. So, my friends and I cycled to the cemetery in the dead of night.

It was at this cemetery that we sat in the dark with only one or two candles, where we drafted our leaflet. Next came the challenge of printing the leaflet. In those days, people used a Gestener cyclostyle machine to reproduce documents. But we had to improvise. We made our own cyclostyling arrangements.

One night, we cycled to the cemetery carrying candles and three packets of legal-size paper; each packet had 200 pages. We had to cut the stencil by writing the leaflet with a stylus nib and then printing it by using ink and a fluorescent light as a tube to make the ink even. In this way, we printed 600 copies of our leaflets!

Next came the problem of distribution because handing the leaflets out openly would mean we would get arrested. So we thought of an innovative way of distributing them. We were six friends and we divided ourselves into four groups. Each group was assigned to distribute the leaflets in different schools or other public places. I was assigned to distribute the leaflet in my school.

I went through the main gate, which did not have a guard in the late evenings. Then I broke the glass and opened the window of the classroom. Once in the classroom, I took a bench, placed it under the fan and stood on the bench to place the leaflets on the blades of the fan. I placed small stones on the leaflets so they would not fall off. The next day, when the students came into class and turned on the fan, the leaflets would fly all over and get distributed!

This seemed a fool proof plan, except that one of our friends decided not to follow our carefully thought-out instructions, and started openly distributing the leaflets. Sure enough, he was arrested, and he revealed all our names under questioning.

The police came to our home and asked for me. My

father asked if he could accompany me, but they said it was not necessary. I could see my father standing at a distance from the police station.

We were first taken to the main Monywa police station and interrogated separately by two police officers. One talked to us softly and kindly, but the other was harsh. This is the well-known carrot and stick method, but this was my first time at a police station.

The harsh policeman put his pistol on the table in front of me and even slapped me once or twice, and punched me. He demanded to know who was behind our plans. At first, I denied everything, but then he produced photos of our friend distributing the leaflet openly. After that, it was impossible for me to deny our actions.

We were taken to the administration building next to the military intelligence office, where we slept in the hall.

The next day, the Monywa University students staged a protest demanding our release. The police and military intelligence called our parents to the police station. They then marched us all, six students and their families, to the Monywa Regional College and produced us before the Principal. The police said since the six of us were not being detained, the demonstration should be withdrawn.

The student leaders agreed to end their protest. The procession, which was to take place with the flag on which I had drawn the fighting peacock, did not happen.

After my release, there was little I could do by way of political activities because the authorities kept up their surveillance. Besides, I had my metric examination to study for. I passed the examination in 1997.

As all the colleges and universities were closed, I asked my parents' permission to go to Yangon. There, I joined a private course in computer science. By this time, my cousin had passed out of Rangoon Institute of Technology and had become an Assistant Engineer in the Public Works

Department (PWD). He lived in Shwe Pyi Tha, a satellite town of Yangon. I stayed with him. Later, I went back to Yangon in 1998 and stayed in rented accommodation.

My cousin would take me to various bookshops and cafes where I heard political discussions. One of these cafes was called Wuthering Heights; no, not after Emily Brontë's book, but a pun on it. The name was given by authors who met there and had stormy discussions, hence the nickname. In Burmese, it was called *Lay Htan Kone*, which when translated meant Wuthering Heights.

I found an interview with the owner of the tea shop published in the *Myanmar Times*, where he explains how the tea shop got its name:

> "When it first opened, Ko Than Thein's tea shop didn't have a name. With all the creative customers around, however, that didn't last long. It was author Min Lu, Ko Than Thein recalled, who first took the Myanmar-language title of the novel Wuthering Heights and used it to name the shop Lay Htan Kone. It's an honour that makes Ko Than Thein proud. "I fell in love with the name he gave," he said. Since its inception, a number of writers and poets have written about Lay Htan Kone tea shop, including Mya Than Tint, who immortalised it in his essay "Tea Shop". As a result, the shop has taken on a new identity among the cultural community, Ko Than Thein said. "In the literary communities, I have seldom seen a person who doesn't know Lay Htan Kone tea shop on 33rd Street."[5]

Then there were many shops which kept photocopied copies of books because most books were banned. These were kept secretly at the back, and only those in the know could buy them.

I read many books at this time and was especially inspired by Mya Than Tint's (1929-1998) book called *Dataung ko Kyaw Ywei, Mee Pinte ko Hpyat Myi*, which translates to *Across the Mountain of Swords and the Sea of Fire*.

Mya Than Tint was a writer who had spent several years

in prison under Gen Ne Win, but he continued to write. He had also translated many English novels to Burmese, including *Gone with the Wind* by Margaret Mitchell in 1939.

I also read novels by Hla Myint, known by his pseudonym Nat Nwe, founder of *Nwe Ni*, a foreign affairs magazine. He was the author of more than 100 novels and translated 20 from other languages into Burmese. I read his novel on the Northern Mountains about the Kachins, *Myanma pyi Myauk pine*.

I read the seven volumes of the American novel *Saigon* by Anthony Grey, published in 1982 and translated by Maung Tun Thu, and I read *Freedom at Midnight* by Larry Collins and Dominique Lapierre about the events surrounding the Indian independence movement and partition. I read the book in its Burmese translation.

Later, in 1997, a writers movement developed, drawing inspiration from the stream of consciousness style of writing of James Joyce and Virginia Woolf. Of course, the contents were Burmese, and unlike the Western writers, their Burmese counterparts were also involved the pro-democracy movement. I was deeply influenced by many of these writers. Zaw Zaw Aung was one of the poets who introduced modern and postmodern literature to the Burmese people. He was born in Monywa.

I was in Yangon from 1997 to the end of 1999. When I returned to Monywa, a friend and I opened a teashop at the Government Technical College. We called our teashop Café 2000.

Soon, the teashop became the rendezvous place for students not only from Monywa but also students who were studying at the Mandalay Institute of Technology. So the teashop became a hub for activists to exchange news and have discussions. We held poetry recitations and celebrated Mother's Day.

We started to notice that our café was under

surveillance. The military must have put pressure on our landlord because he refused to renew his lease with us. In any case, the university had opened, so I joined classes at the university.

In 2000, the Government opened colleges and universities all over the country, and we from Monywa did not have to go to Mandalay or Yangon to study. I joined the college where they were teaching Computer Science. The Computer Science College stood in the middle of a paddy field very near the famous massive Buddha statue. We were around 300 students, and there were only 20 computers with no access to the internet. So I shifted to Monywa University, where they were offering a new subject—Psychology. I took that course, but we had two young teachers and almost no books, even in the library. I was very disappointed, but managed to graduate in 2004.

However, in 2003, I was witness to a very important political event involving an assassination attempt on Daw Aung San Suu Kyi.

Depayin Massacre of May 30, 2003

Daw Aung San Suu Kyi had been put under house arrest for 15 years altogether, but in between, she would be released and then again detained. In May 2002, she was released, and she toured all parts of the country along with her supporters.

In May 2003, she announced she would be coming to Monywa. We were all excited, and a local member of the NLD asked me to help with her security arrangements. I readily agreed.

We were all waiting for Daw Aung San Suu Kyi to arrive. It was very late in the evening when she finally arrived at Monywa. In those days, there were long and frequent power cuts, and so many candle factories had sprung up. On that day, the factories distributed candles freely, so when Daw Aung San Suu Kyi entered Monywa, everyone was standing with lighted candles. It was a stunning sight to behold—three to four miles of lit candles.

The next day, Daw Aung San Suu Kyi offered alms at the local monastery and set off. I was behind her car in a jeep when it suddenly broke down. I had to move to the back of her motorcade, which consisted of 1,000 motorcycles and at least a hundred cars. The security agencies cut off the motorcade, and I was left at a place near Ahlone Myo near the Zawtika and Okkan monasteries. I called the monks from the two monasteries to join us, and I requested the commander to remove the barriers. The commander refused, the security personnel took photos of us and ordered the crowd to disperse. When we refused to disperse, he gave orders to shoot at us at around 7 pm. A student from GTC Monywa was killed in the firing.

I did not see the massacre of the NLD leaders who had gone ahead.

The next day, I had to flee from my home and take shelter as a novice at a monastery in Kyaung Paw village, Yinmbain Township, across Chindwin River. I was finally arrested on a false drug case. This was a common method that the authorities used to frame political activists, including the MP of Monywa, Nyunt Aung. He managed to get his sentences converted from death sentence to a life sentence. Later, President U Thein gave amnesty to many political prisoners.

That day, Daw Aung San Suu Kyi had managed to escape because of her driver's skills. She had escaped a similar attempted assassination in 1996. This time, at least 70 NLD members and supporters were killed, and many were injured when their convoy was attacked.

According to many reports, the assassination attempt was well planned. According to U Aung Htoo, General Secretary, Burma Lawyers' Council, Thailand:[6]

(a) The Dyna and Tolargi trucks, carrying about 1,000 attackers, tailed Daw Aung San Suu Kyi's convoy before they reached the killing field where the crime was to be committed.

(b) Around that first killing field, another 3,000 attackers were waiting in clumps of bushes and thickets beside the road in the dark of night.

(c) Bogus monks wrapped red cloths around their arms to prevent mistaken attacks and make them distinct from the monks who had accompanied Daw Aung San Suu Kyi's convoy.

(d) First, 1,000 attackers started to attack the Kyi villagers and supporters of Daw Aung San Suu Kyi at the rear of her convoy.

(e) Then, almost at the same time, the 3,000 attackers waiting in readiness joined the attack and battered all people in Daw Aung San Suu Kyi's convoy.

(f) Another 1,000 attackers were also waiting with barricades at the second killing field, about ten minutes from the first one. Those attackers assaulted all motorcycles and cars that escaped from the first killing field.

(g) At the two killing fields, the headlights of Dyna trucks were arranged by the authorities to light the areas. At the second killing field, spotlights were set up in the big trees beside the road.

I was in Monywa jail for three years from 2004 to 2007. In jail, I met many other student activists, including Maung Maung Oo from Mandalay, who was given two life sentences. There was Chit Thein Tun Oo, who was given a five-year sentence. He was released in 2010 when the President pardoned several political prisoners. Chit Thein Tun became a monk and went to live in Maha Myaing Monastery in the middle of thick forests. I came back to Monywa to continue my studies.

The Saffron Revolution

I was released in 2007, a month before the Saffron

Revolution—the biggest uprising 1988. Described as such because of the participation of several thousand saffron-clad monks, the Saffron Revolution was triggered by the government's act of raising fuel prices by 500 per cent.

On 22 September, a crowd of 2,000 monks and civilians walked past a roadblock and gathered outside Daw Aung San Suu Kyi's house. She came out to greet and pray with the Buddhist monks outside her gate. This was the first time she had been seen in public since 2003. The rally was a strong and clear display of unity between the monks and the pro-democracy movement.

Over 100,000 monks and ordinary citizens were marching in Yangon, and demonstrations were taking place in every state and division in Burma.

In Monywa, home to many large monasteries, some of which have 2,000 students studying scriptures, around 3000 to 4,000 monks came out and marched in the streets. There were around 20,000 supporters who gathered in the streets in their support. People brought snacks and cold drinks for the monks.

I had just been released from jail just a few weeks before, and I too joined the protestors. I also took about 20 cartons of one-litre bottles of Dragon-brand water from my parents' restaurant and distributed it among the monks as they marched in a long processions over three or four days.

The military commander in charge of the region was Thar Aye, and he was a staunch supporter of the junta. He did not shoot or arrest the monks, but he targeted the people supporting the monks. He arrested many people who came to join the protest. Since I had just been released from jail, I thought it would be safer to go away to Yangon for some time.

I stayed in a rented room along with friends who had come with me from Monywa. This was already the end of 2007.

Cyclone Nargis

While I was in Yangon, I joined a course in photojournalism at a private institute. It was soon after that that Cyclone Nargis hit the coast of Myanmar in May 2008, causing massive devastation.

It is estimated that at least 2.4 million people were severely affected by the cyclone. Structural damage throughout Myanmar was extensive, causing over a million people to become homeless after the calamity. The people living in the Irrawaddy Delta were the most badly affected.

It was estimated that 84,000 people had died in the town of Labutta alone. I joined the search and rescue operations in that town. It was there that I met the comedian, Maung Thura, better known as Zarganar (Tweezers). He too had come to join in the search and rescue operations.

I knew that the comedian was a trained dentist and that his parents were famous writers. Zarganar (also spelt as Zaganar) was born in 1961 and was known as a fierce critic of the junta. He was best known for his wicked puns against the military. He had been banned from performing publicly.

Soon after I met him in Labutta, Zarganar was arrested in June 2008 for speaking to the foreign media about the critical situation of millions of people left homeless by Cyclone Nargis. He was sentenced to 59 years in prison, though the sentence was reduced to 24 years. He was sent to a prison in the Kachin state in the far north of the country. Fortunately, he did not have to serve his full sentence because he was released along with many political prisoners under a Presidential amnesty in 2011.[7]

As a photojournalist, I took photos of the scenes of the devastation caused by Cyclone Nargis. I still remember the dead bodies lying there, giving off a strong stench. The memory of the floating, rotting bodies continues to haunt me.

I contacted local agencies and individuals for the relief efforts because the junta did not allow UN aid agencies to enter the country. The military did not want the world to see the devastation. Since I was taking photos and sending them to the media, I came under their scrutiny. So I left for Yangon, where I had to move from house to house to avoid being arrested.

During this period, I managed to be trained as a chef at the famous five-star hotel, the Kandawgyi Palace Hotel. But perhaps more importantly, I also learnt something about internet café services. In 2009, when I returned to Monywa, I decided to open an internet café in my hometown.

In the midst of the search and rescue operations, the military conducted a referendum—considered by many to have been rigged—and managed to get the 2008 Constitution passed. The Constitution guaranteed the military 25 per cent of the seats in Parliament. I did not bother to vote in the referendum.

My Internet Cafe

There were around 15 to 20 internet cafes in Monywa. There was no WIFI at the time. The internet connection was slow, using, as it did, the Asymmetric Digital Subscriber Line (better known as ADSL). We still used landlines (though by 2007, we had 3G). People did not have mobiles or laptops, so these internet cafes flourished.

The majority of people who came to my café would make video calls to their relatives, working as migrant workers in Thailand, Malaysia and Japan. These calls through the internet were cheap, compared to the telephone-based overseas calls they had had to make earlier.

I helped my café patrons open their Facebook accounts and taught them how to make passwords for their Gmail accounts, etc.

By now, Facebook had become very popular among the

youth. And by 2010, the youth that came to my café were into gaming. For my part, I was making a lot of money subletting the WIFI connection at the internet café.

In 2010, the military announced elections, but the NLD decided not to participate. Both sides, the military and the NLD, used social media to disseminate their views.

The military, which had not yet realized the power of social media and its huge reach, did not try to control its use. After all, there were no fibre optics and people did not have mobiles. However, when we applied for a license to run an internet café, we had to sign a bond stating that our patrons would not use the premises for political activities and if anyone was caught using it for such purposes, we—the café owners—would have to report them to the authorities.

The ignorance of authorities about the workings of the internet was frankly quite amusing. There was a story about how Zarganar, who when asked by a judge to provide details of his email account, enraged him by correctly giving him his username; the judge believed email was like old-fashioned letters and that the comedian was mocking the judiciary by giving him what he perceived as false information.

Impact of Social Media

In 2012, by-elections were announced, and Daw Aung San Suu Kyi decided to contest the elections. Till then, only the ruling Union Solidarity and Development Party (USDP), had access to the internet in their office and in government-run libraries. When the NLD decided to contest all 43 seats in the by-elections they realized they too needed internet access.

I immediately offered my services to the NLD. The Parliamentary seat in Monywa had not fallen vacant, so the NLD candidate, Khin San Hlaing, contested from Pale, west of the River Chindwin. Khin San Hlaing had won the 1990 elections when the junta had not allowed the NLD to form a government. Now she was standing for elections again.

Many people opposed her candidacy because she was considered an outsider to the region. However, I offered to drive her around the constituency and also serve as the NLD Information Officer.

On the final day of the election campaign, I called a friend who was an expert in using social media; they managed to use WIFI to live broadcast the election news. The NLD candidate won.

Copper Mine Protests, 2012

There is a large copper mine complex across the river from Monywas at Letpadaung. The mining operation are run by a joint venture company, comprising Wanbao Mining Ltd., a subsidiary of Chinese state-owned Norinco, and the Myanmar Economic Holding Co. (MEHC), controlled by the junta.

The project was started in 2010. One of the people active in the protests against this company because of the environmental pollution it was causing, was the poet Kay Za Win, a Buddhist monk for much of his adult life, till the coming of the Spring Revolution.

The mining necessitated the eviction of many local farmers; the mining itself had caused extensive ecological damage in the area. Now that the military had started making reforms and granting people more room for protests, the people collected together and set up six camps.

The protests had been going on for several days, when on 29 November 2012, the police arrived to disperse the protestors.

I had gone to join the protestors and to take photos. I saw truckloads of police arrive. They spread out to the area and started firing what was then described as "firebombs." In fact, they were military-issue white phosphorus grenades, which cause burns and are not allowed on civilian populations.

I saw how the white phosphorus had caused severe burns even as I ferried 20 monks from the site to the hospital in Monywa.

The police denied using incendiary bombs—they insisted that they had only used smoke bombs and tear gas—but I had collected evidence from the residue in the shell.

The government accused the protestors of damaging the country's reputation. It arrested at least six activists, who were then sent to the notorious Insein prison on charges of defaming the nation. Disappointingly, Aung San Suu Kyi refused to speak for the protestors. In the end, a Commission of Enquiry was set up, headed by Aung San Suu Kyi, with MP Khin San a member of the Commission.

The Commission gave its findings by March 2013, in which it basically whitewashed the whole incident in order to please both the Chinese and the junta.[8] I had examined the cannisters myself and seen the burn wounds on the monks, so I knew the report was a cover-up.

Meanwhile, I had sent my photos to many in the media, but one journalist published them without giving me credit. He even got a prize for his coverage, though the award was withdrawn when it was discovered that the photos were mine.

Between 2012 to 2015, the government was still controlled by the military, so we cannot say we were living under democratic rule. The time for the 2015 elections was nearing, and the NLD would be standing this time. Would we, the people of Burma, finally live under a democratic society?

By this time, I had felt a need to have my independent source of income. I opened a restaurant called FOTO in 2013. I called it FOTO because I put up my photos in the restaurant. The restaurant was my home as well; I slept there. And no, I did not consult any astrologer before naming my restaurant!

2015 Elections

I was very active during this period in the campaigning. This was also the time I got to work closely with the 88 generation. The 88 Generation had formed the "Peace and Open Society" and were travelling around the country. I met them in Monywa, and began working as a photojournalist with them.

The 88 generation was open to supporting Aung San Suu Kyi and her party, the NLD, and so when she asked them to give her a list of candidates, they provided the names of about 15 to 20 candidates. The list included many famous student leaders who had been recently released from jail.

The NLD even asked the local units of their party to give them names of candidates. In the end, however, it was the party at Yangon which made the decision. The NLD only fielded three candidates of the 88 generation. It was one of these candidates who later turned traitor and became a witness for the prosecution where he provided false testimony that he had given Aung San Suu Kyi 11.2 kgs of gold.

By this time, most people had mobiles and their own access to the internet, so I had closed down my internet café. However, I was active on Facebook and had some 100,000 followers. As a way of supporting the NLD, I lampooned the military and wrote satirical pieces. This got me into trouble.

For you to understand my cartoon, you must know a little of the history of this part of Myanmar. Kokang is a part of the Shan state on the Myanmar-China border. The Communist Party of Burma was active in this area, but after

1989, the military had taken control and made Kokang an autonomous First Special Region in the Shan state. The Shan rebels took control of the region and signed a ceasefire with Myanmar's armed forces. The rebels called themselves the Myanmar National Democratic Alliance Army (MNDA). In 2015, there were several clashes between the MNDA and the Myanmar Army in which the rebels were defeated, and martial law was imposed.[9]

The junta celebrates this victory in its propaganda material. It was this victory that I lampooned by calling the Kokang battle a "condom battle". I also made fun of the logo of the North East Command, which was a half rising sun. I portrayed it as a fried egg.

The junta was not amused.

My Arrest

One day in March 2015, the police filed an FIR against me under Section 5(a) of the Emergency Provisions Act of 1950.[10]

The section reads:

Whoever does anything with any of the following intent; that is to say:

> To depreciate, pervert, hinder, restrain, or vandalise the loyalty, enthusiasm, acquiescence, health, training, or performance of duties of the army organisations of the Union or of civil servants in a way that would induce their respect for the government to be diminished, or to disobey rules, or to be disloyal to the government;

Many political prisoners had been arrested under this law and given long prison sentences.

Soon after the FIR against me was registered, a combined force of the police, military, and intelligence agencies raided my parents' restaurant and quickly covered our CCTVs. Then they started searching the restaurant and took away my laptop, mobile and the hard disk of the CCTV.

They arrested me and took me straight to Mandalay, where I was interrogated by the military intelligence. I was, then, brought back to Monywa and produced before a magistrate. When I asked the magistrate why I was being charged, she said she had no idea and that she had been told by the police to open the case against me.

She directed the police to take me into judicial custody. I was imprisoned in Monywa to await trial and possibly a long prison sentence. I knew several people who had died in prison. Besides, political prisoners were seldom given access to lawyers, and if they were formally charged, they would be tried in a closed trial where no one had access.

Knowing this, I had secretly handed over a piece of paper with the phone numbers of some of the leaders of the 88 generation and a few reporters and asked my mother to call them after they took me away. She must have done that because the next day, media outlets covered the story of my arrest. Many 88 generation student leaders called for my release. They staged a 'Free Aung Nay Myo' campaign on social media. The Myanmar Journalist Network (MJN) and Myanmar Press Council (MPC) also issued statements, condemning my arbitrary arrest and demanding my immediate release.

Upon my release, the police returned my laptop and other equipment after deleting all the data on my laptop, computer, and mobile phone. I was able to restore only about one third of the data. I lost my Facebook account with 100,000 followers.

My 88 generation friends took me back with them to Yangon so I could be relatively safe.

The Long March

In Yangon, I found myself in the midst of the student protests.

From 2012 to 2015, General Thein Sein initiated some

reforms, such as releasing political prisoners and giving the media more freedom. But under the guise of reform, the government acquired more powers to control the people.

Over 50 years of military rule in Myanmar formally ended in 2011, and under a new quasi-civilian government, the country opened up to the world. In 2014, the military-backed government introduced the National Education Law, under which, existing student unions would be outlawed and replaced with state-sponsored (and controlled) student and teacher associations.

The students opposed the new law and when the government did not heed their demands, decided to march from Mandalay to Yangon, a distance of nearly 600 kilometres. They never reached their final destination, as they were beaten and rounded up in Letpadan while they were preparing to proceed on their journey. All of them were arrested there. Among those who marched was my friend, Wai Moe Naing, who was President of the Monywa Students Union that year. I supported him financially at the time. The poet Kay Za Win was also among the protestors.

In Yangon, the students protested in support of their demand for a repeal of the new education laws, and I also joined the demonstrations. At one of these demonstrations, I met Nilar Thein, the wife of the famous student leader known as Ko Jimmy. Nilar Thein herself was a political prisoner for many years, and it was in prison that they fell in love.

I went back to Monywa and campaigned for the NLD. At one point, I handed the NLD flags to the rickshaw puller, and for that, I was hauled by the police and released only after signing a bond stating I would not break the law: they said I had not asked for permission to hand out flags to the rickshaw pullers.

On the day of the election, I was in Monywa as an election observer. I ferried the NLD members from their office to the polling booths, and of course, I was excited when the NLD won. But I also had started seeing certain authoritarian tendencies within the party, so I distanced myself from political parties. However I made one exception and that was for Ko Ko Gyi. Ko Ko Gyi was one of the most prominent student leaders from the 88 generation, who had spent many years in prison till he was finally released in 2012. Ko Ko Gyi had expected to stand for elections in the 2015 elections as an NLD candidate, but was not given a ticket. In 2018, he decided to launch his own party called the People Party. He asked me to help him open a branch in Monywa. I did help him but did not become a member of his party or any other party.[11]

I stayed on in Monywa and occupied myself in charitable works. I helped an elderly Burman nun open a home for old people, and I distributed milk porridge and boiled eggs to the patients at the Monywa hospital.

Criticism of NLD

I had opened another Facebook page where I posted my criticism of the local NLD party leaders for nepotism. In 2017, one of the NLD leaders filed a case against me under the notorious Section 66(d) of the Telecommunication Act. I joined the campaign for repealing this notorious law, led by a poet called Maung Saung Kha.

The Telecommunication Act was passed in 2013 by the former Thein Sein government. Section 66(d) was used to restrict peaceful speech for political reasons.

Section 66(d) is a criminal law provision that permits penalties of up to three years in prison for "extorting, coercing, restraining wrongfully, defaming, disturbing, causing undue influence or threatening any person using a telecommunications network." Use of the law had soared since the new NLD government took office in 2015, with at least 54 people charged with violating the law and at least eight people sentenced to prison terms to date, almost all for postings on Facebook or other social media.

With mounting criticism, the NLD-led government did introduce amendments to the section. When Section 66(d) was first introduced in 2013, it permitted anyone to file a complaint that a particular communication had violated the law. Most of the defamation complaints have not been filed by the person allegedly defamed, but by others who were or claimed to be offended by the statement.

In 2017 the Section 66(d) amended the law and allowed judges to release on bail those charged under the law. Only people directly affected by an alleged offence, or those with the permission of an affected person, could now press charges under the amended law. Ironically, there were more people arrested under this law under the NLD-led government than under the previous government. Some reports said close to 100 people were arrested under this law during the NLD Government.

Fortunately, I was released after signing a bond. I mention this to explain why I had become disillusioned with the NLD, and I chose to stay away from party politics. I continued my social work, which gave me much more satisfaction.

I also did not like the way the NLD imposed their ideology on the ethnic nationalities by installing the bust of Gen Aung San in Kayah state, where the people wanted to install their own heroes. They did the same thing in the Naga self-administered township of Khampti. Further, the NLD government cut off internet in the Rakhine state in 2019.

Tattoo as Resistance

By now, tattoos had become very popular among young people in Myanmar. Of course, tattooing is not new to our culture. Many ethnic groups, including the Shan, Karen and Bama, have used tattoos as a distinguishing cultural marker and a symbol of strength, courage. Tattoos are painful and permanent.

In Monywa, I initiated a *WeLoveTattoo* campaign and also involved the youth in activities such as tree planting. I decided to get together with many of the youth who had tattoos, even though their tattoos were not political. These youth had tattoos of dragons and symbols they had seen on gangsters in movies.

In 2021, after the coup, we joined the national tattoo campaign when tattoo artists gave free tattoos to people. These tattoo artists sat by the roadside and tattooed the three finger salute, portraits of Daw Aung San Suu Kyi or the words "Spring Revolution" on volunteers.

Coup in 2021

I was in Monywa when the military announced a coup on 1 February 2021. The next day, we started changing our profile on Facebook to black as a mark of protest. On that day, we found a message circulating that said that we should not protest for the next 72 hours, because if we did, the UN would not support us. This may have been a part of the military's psychological operations (PSYOPS).

I had a zoom meeting with the student leader, Wai Moe Naing, who was at the time in Yangon, on what I should do in Monywa. Wai Moe Naing had emerged as our leader in Monywa and had popularized the idea of banging pots and pans.

Wai Moe Niang came back on 5 February whereupon we organized a procession of motorcycles honking loudly in protest against the coup. This was the beginning of the Spring Revolution in Monywa. There was not a day when we did not bring out processions on the streets of our town.

On 3 March, I was right in front of a procession. Those who led the procession wore gas masks and carried shields made of iron and had yellow helmets. Behind us were the flagbearers, and then came the general public. That day, as on so many other days, the poet Kay Zar Win was among the demonstrators. The police opened fire as we reached Pagoda Road. It was the first day we faced a military crackdown in which nine people were killed. Among them was the poet. I think he was targeted by a sniper standing on top of one of the buildings. The police dragged his body through the street, along the blood-stained asphalt, before throwing him into a van. I helped take the nine bodies to the hospital.

The people made a ring of flowers to mark the place where the poet's body had fallen.

It was becoming very dangerous to organize demonstrations, so we decided to have processions of scooters and motorcycles.

After this, Wai Moe Niang and I went into hiding. The police came looking for me at 2 am and again at 4 am. They put up vinyl posters with our faces and announced that we were wanted. They pasted the posters at busy crossroads and even made announcements on their TV station. They raided my restaurant and sealed it.

On 15 April, Wai Moe Naing was arrested. The military used an unmarked vehicle to ram Wai Moe Naing while he was driving on a moped as part of our protest rally of two-wheelers. When he tried to escape on foot, a group of armed men disembarked and assaulted him and a female protester before detaining them both.

Under these circumstances, it was dangerous to stay on in Monywa, so I went across the Chindwin River and stayed in the villages and then returned to Monywa to try and organize a demonstration, but found that the repression was so severe that I decided to leave Monywa and take refuge in India.

I went to Chin state and contacted the Chin National

Army. They helped me, along with two MPs, to cross into Mizoram, India in April 2021. On the border, we had to be checked for Covid-19. Till then, I had barely heard of Covid because it had not spread so much in Myanmar at the time.

We were then taken to a refugee camp in Mizoram. I missed Monywa and felt sad that I had to leave my home and the struggle. Although the Mizoram government gave us shelter and food, it was not easy living in the camp. There was water scarcity—we got two small buckets of water to wash, and the meals were invariably rice, dal and potatoes.

I stayed in Mizoram for one and a half years. I got a job as a news presenter and anchor at the National Unity Government (NUG) television. I continued my work as a photojournalist. I received news that my parents were arrested on 18 December 2022 after the army saw me on NUG TV.

I did not feel very safe working at the border, so I decided to go to New Delhi. I arrived in Delhi in December 2023 and have been living there ever since, working for NUG TV and among the other Burmese refugees in India.

I Decide to Have a Tattoo

Away from Monywa and from my people, with thoughts of those who are in jail and those who are involved in armed resistance, I wanted to find a way of protesting and also expressing my love and commitment to the Spring Revolution. I decided to have the milestones of the Spring Revolution tattooed on my body as a way of expressing my total and permanent commitment.

I contacted a famous tattoo artist, Chin Ley, who is a Chin and a graduate of the Mandalay Fine Art Academy. He had been a part of the Spring Revolution. I thought he would be the right person to tattoo my back.

Let me describe my tattoo.

Across my shoulders are the two words: SPRING

REVOLUTION. Then there are stars, I do not remember exactly how many, but they represent the fallen martyrs of the Spring Revolution.

On my left shoulder is Zeya Thaw, my hero.

His full name was Phyo Zeya Thaw (26 March 1981-23 July 2022). Zeya Thaw was younger than me. I had first met him when he accompanied Aung San Suu Kyi to Monywa just before the Depayin massacre of 2003. I also met him during his concerts and I loved his music. His band, Acid, was very popular. In 2000, it released the first hip hop album in Myanmar. It topped the Burmese charts and stayed there a long time. A reporter from the Democratic Voice of Burma described his music as blending a "combative, angry style with indigenous poeticism". His songs spoke of the hardships faced by the Burmese people and were critical of the regime.

Zeya Thaw also did a lot of charity work. At one concert, he teamed with poets Saw Wai and Aung Way to raise money for a charity for HIV-positive orphans founded by the comedian Zarganar. Along with fellow rapper Nge Nge, he also visited Zarganar's orphanages to help teach English to the children.

Zeya Thaw was one of four founding members of Generation Wave, a youth movement opposed to the military's State Peace and Development Council. The group was founded on 9 October 2007 after the Saffron Revolution. The group had anti-government stickers and circulated anti-government films, including Rambo (fourth in the series), released in 2008, in which the titular character battles Tatmadaw (Myanmar military) soldiers in Karen state. The film gave a boost to the Karen resistance forces fighting the Burmese army for decades. One line from the film became very popular: "Live for nothing, or die for something" as a rallying point and battle cry. The film was banned by the junta.

In 2008, he was arrested and sentenced to five years. Many members of his group were also arrested. He was released in 2011. The following year he stood for elections as an NLD candidate and won. He was one of the youngest members of the 2012 Pyithu Hluttaw, the lower house of the Myanmar Parliament.

After the coup Ko Phyo Zeya Thaw was arrested on 18 November 2021, sentenced to death by a military court two months later on 21 January 2022. He was executed on 23 July along with 88 Generation student leader, Ko Jimmy, and two other democracy activists, Ko Hla Myo Aung and Ko Aung Thu Zaw.

Below the figure of Zeya Thaw is a smaller figure in grey. It is a young woman wearing trousers and a shirt with a backpack. This young girl's name is Kyal Sin, who was popularly known as Angel. She was ethnic Chinese; her Chinese name was Deng Jiaxi. She died on 3 March 2021, after a sniper shot her in the head. That day, 60 people died; she was the youngest, barely 20 years old.

Angel was a taekwando instructor and champion. And she worked as a singer and dancer.

On the day of her death, she was wearing a T-shirt with the phrase "Everything will be OK".

Her friend Myat Thu told Reuters that Kyal Sin kicked open a water pipe so protesters could wash tear gas from their eyes. This was minutes before she was shot in the head. Thousands of people attended her funeral.

*****

Opposite the figure of Angel is the figure of Dr Tayzar San, who led the first anti-military junta protests in Mandalay. It is said he began the Spring Revolution. He is one of the most wanted by the junta, but for now is safe and is a member of the National Unity Consultative Council (NUCC).

I knew him personally and had organized his talk show in Myanmar.

Facing Zeya Thaw, there is a figure of a woman wearing a hat and spectacles. She is holding a microphone and giving a speech. This is Thinzar Hein, who was a second-year nursing student in Monywa. She had left her home against her parents' wishes to join the movement against military rule.

The tattoo is based on the photo of her giving a speech in front of Monywa's clock tower on 22 February, the day of the "five twos" (22/2/2021) general strike and the beginning of the Spring Revolution.

She told the meeting that her father was a member of the Union Solidarity and Development Party, the junta-backed party, which had been defeated in the 2020 elections. Her father opposed her decision to join the civil disobedience movement, forcing her to she walk out of her home and live with a friend, Aye Aye (not her real name).

Thinzar Hein used her formal medical training to teach others how to tend to the wounded. On 28 March 2021, she was shot while attending to the injured. She was just 20 years old. Ma Thinzar Hein left a note on Facebook, "I am walking a path and uncertain of returning home, please forgive me, loved ones."

The day she was killed, Aye Aye was also shot in her shoulder. She continues to be a part of the civil disobedience movement.

The military junta has killed hundreds of medical workers.

Between Zeya Thaw and Thinzar Hein is a map of Myanmar. And below that is Daw Aung San Suu Kyi caught in the iron grip of the military, but instead of where the head of the military ruler should be is the proud three finger salute, the symbol of our Spring Revolution.

Then there are two people looking at each other. The person on the left is my beloved friend Wai Moe Naing facing me. He was born in a Muslim family. His father had died when he was very young, and his mother, Moe Sandar Kyu, was a school teacher.

He began writing as a student, with his first short story being published in *Teen Magazine* at the age of 13. His writings have since been published in several literary outlets, including *Khit Yanantthit Magazine* and *Pae Tin Tharn Journal*.

Wai Moe Naing was President of the Monywa University Student Union from 2014 to 2015, and a member of Monywa's General Strike Committee and the Sagaing Regional Youth Committee.

When an unidentified vehicle hit him, he was injured and left unattended. He was beaten and tortured inside jail and put in solitary confinement. He has been sentenced to 74 years in prison.

He and I worked closely, and that is why I had the tattoo of both of us facing each other.

*****

On my right shoulder is the tattoo of Ko Kyaw Min Yu, better known as Ko Jimmy (1969-2022). Ko Jimmy was destined to live a great life in which he fought for the people. As a 19-year-old student, he started his mission to free Myanmar from its evil rulers. At the age of 53, he became a martyr when he was hanged along with Zeya Thaw on 23 July 2022.

Ko Jimmy had spent many years in jail, and while in prison, he wrote several books. He wrote the self-help book *Making Friends*, which became a bestseller, in 2005. In 2012, he published a novel, *The Moon in Inle Lake*, which had been written in 2010 during a prison sentence in Taunggyi. While serving a sentence in Taunggyi, he wrote several political post-modern short stories that were published in Japan under the pen name Pan Pu Lwin Pyin. Ko Jimmy translated numerous novels, including The Da Vinci Code, while in prison.

Ko Jimmy met his wife when she was in jail. When they came out of jail, they got married and had a baby. Ko Jimmy was arrested again when the baby was just four months old.

I met him several times when he was working in the Peace and Open Society. I was deeply influenced by his courage and dignity.

There are other smaller tattoos, such as of a child—because so many children have been killed—and of people holding placards. I want to tattoo every milestone in our movement; it is my way of showing my love for the revolution and my permanent commitment to its goals.

It took 12 days for my body to be tattooed. Chin Ley, the tattoo artist, had one Indian assistant, and for the first four days, they would tattoo for eight hours a day. Then, for 8 days, they would tattoo for three hours a day.

On my lower back are the words "Fuck Military Rule 1/2/2021." This expresses my deep anger, rage against the way the military crushed the dreams of so many young people.

I intend to continue tattooing my entire body with all the future milestones in our Spring Revolution. I know we can defeat the brutal army rule.

What about the future?

We will discuss that after we have won. We have a long way to go. I know there are pockets of Buddhist chauvinists who pose a threat to our future, and there are very real divisions in our society but the Spring Revolution has brought us together and I think we can dream of a good future.

NOTES

1. https://www.burmalibrary.org/sites/burmalibrary.org/files/obl/docs22/Tee-Noe_Karen-Resistance-Poetry_Trans-and-Intro-by-Violet-Cho.pdf

2. https://insightmyanmar.org/burmadhammablog/2021/3/8/not-until-the-end-of-the-world
3. SLORC formed after the 1988 uprising and in 1997 the name was changed to State Peace and Development Council.
4. Amnesty International, Myanmar September-December 1996
5. *Myanmar Times* July 15-21, 2013 https://www.burmalibrary.org/sites/burmalibrary.org/files/obl/docs15/MT686-2013-07-21-op-red.pdf
6. http://www.humanrights.asia/resources/journals-magazines/article2/special-edtion-the-depayin-massacre-burma/the-depayin-massacre-a-crime-against-humanity-and-its-effect-on-national-reconciliation/
7. Zarganar was awarded the Lillian Hellman and Dashiell Hammett Award by the Fund for Free Expression, a committee organized by the New York-based Human Rights Watch. In October 2008, Zarganar was awarded One Humanity Award by PEN Canada of which he is an honorary member.
8. https://www.charltonsmyanmar.com/letpadaung-investigation-commission-issues-final-report/
9. In 2024 the pro-democracy ethnic armed organisation (EAO) of Myanmar took over control of the entire Kokang region in the Shan state bordering China's Yunnan Province, including control of Laukkaing, the principal township of Kokang.
10. The NLD-led Government repealed this law in 2016
11. Ko Ko Gyi has announced that he would stand for elections in the 2025 elections and is willing to engage with the military junta.

Afterword: Thoughts on the Future

Interview with Soe Myint, Editor-in-Chief, *Mizzima Media*

When I asked Aung Nay Myo what he thought the future of Myanmar would look like he said "people would decide after the Spring Revolution had succeeded in defeating the Myanmar military regime."

As of now the armed resistance has succeeded in taking control of more than 50 per cent of the territory. The National Unity Government has been involved in both humanitarian assistance and trying to rebuild villages. The various ethnic nationalities too are having conversations on what kind of democracy and federalism they would want after the end of military rule.

However, no party, organization or leader has emerged who can command the respect of all the people. The international community is pressing the various armed groups to negotiate with the military regime which has announced elections in December 2025; an election which both the armed resistance and the civil disobedience movement have called a sham.

Daw Aung San Suu Kyi is now 80 years old and in prison with serious health issues. The situation inside the country is dire and there is an urgent need for humanitarian aid.

One of the many groups involved in reaching humanitarian assistance to the people inside the country is Soe Myint, the Managing Director and Editor in Chief of

Mizzima Media. He belongs to the 1988 generation and was one of the student activists who hijacked the Thai Airways and diverted it to Kolkata. He founded *Mizzima* while living as a refugee in India. In 2003, he was acquitted in the hijacking case. In 2012 *Mizzima* was the first media-in-exile to go to Myanmar and establish an independent media. But in 2021, after the coup, he took *Mizzima* into the jungles on the Thai-Myanmar border to broadcast from there.[1]

I asked him to give some perspective on the Spring Revolution:

What is the situation inside Myanmar and what kind of humanitarian crisis are the people facing ?

The present situation inside Myanmar is dominated by two interrelated matters. One, the anticipated general election to be held at the end of 2025 and early 2026. And two, the offensive push by junta forces to regain ground ahead of said elections in a bid to offer the elections a further façade of legitimacy.

The elections, scheduled to commence on 28 December, will garner little interest from most Burmese, while opposition groups have already declared them to be a total sham. The NLD, victorious in the 2020 elections prior to the coup, is disqualified from partaking in the 2025 polling. But that is beside the point. Myanmar's generals, and Chinese leaders as well, are looking to the election to bolster the legitimacy of the Nay Pyi Taw government. Recent cosmetic changes to the regime, including its name change, are all part of a broader programme to reap some semblance of legitimacy through the planned end-of-year elections.

Regarding recent offensives by junta forces, this comprises numerous offensive pushes launched since the start of July. Regions of Myanmar subject to these counter attacks include Karenni State, Karen State, and Kachin State, along with the central Myanmar regions of Mandalay, Sagaing, Magway, and Bago. While it is too early to know how lasting any regime gains may be, the uptick in military operations are surely meant to coincide with the run-up to the end-of-year polling.

However, the situation still remains critical for regime forces, not only in the areas of the country already mentioned, but also in Rakhine state, which holds a critical piece to the current crisis in the form of the deep sea port at Kyaukphyu, currently being besieged by local opposition forces. As for Rakhine state itself, reports say the Arakan Army controls 14 of the 17 townships.

What kind of humanitarian assistance has so far been offered by the international community and has it been able to reach the people affected?

Consensus is that there is a growing humanitarian emergency in much of Myanmar, a fact that has only been compounded in the wake of the devastating 28 March earthquake with its epicentre in central Myanmar. According to the UN, nearly 22 million people in Myanmar, out of a total population of 57 million, are in need of humanitarian assistance, while more than 3.5 million have been displaced by the conflict.

While considerable aid has reached the people of Myanmar, it has been nowhere near the amount needed. For example, less than a quarter of UNICEF's 2024 appeal for Myanmar was met. And, of course, the flow and distribution of aid has been hampered by actions of the junta, as they attempt to weaponize the subject of aid.

Regarding support from the international community, the EU, India, US, UN, international NGOs, and others have all contributed aid, though the impact of US intervention has been hampered by the significant budget and staff cuts announced for USAID in early 2025. Additionally, international attention to Myanmar has been hurt by the focus of many traditional donors being on the ongoing conflicts in Ukraine and the Middle East.

India contributed earthquake emergency aid after March 2025 for the people in Sagaing region, who were affected by the earthquake while we also received some medicines and hygiene kits from international donors for the earthquake affected populations in Myanmar.

And then of course there are the obstacles put in place by the junta that impede access to aid. This includes blocking access to conflict-affected areas, alleged attacks on aid workers, the imposition of significant bureaucratic hurdles, and the denial of authorization for certain organizations to operate in certain areas of the country.

What can India do to help rebuild the villages devastated in the natural disasters and the aerial bombing?

There are many things that India can do, albeit in a very challenging environment. But the relative success of India in delivering aid after the March 2025 earthquake proves that India possesses the means to provide much needed aid to help in the rebuilding process. This includes the Indian military delivering essential relief materials as well as the provision of technical and engineering experts to assist in reconstruction plans, though such initiatives likely require the consent of Nay Pyi Taw and would have to go through "official" channels.

However, India can also—working with local governments and civil society groups—ensure access to cross-border relief convoys accessing areas of central and western Myanmar not under junta control. And building on this, New Delhi can further enhance its engagement with non-state actors, recognizing that anti-regime forces now control large parts of the border region. This will in turn further support the delivery of aid and rebuilding efforts in these areas.

India can also contribute in reconstruction of the areas in Chin, Rakhine, Sagaing, Magwe and Kachin which border India in road construction, agriculture, education and health for the local populations in these areas which are now controlled by resistance forces in Myanmar.

It is significant that the EAO and PDF are together resisting and also there is a strong civil disobedience movement both online and offline. But the divisions within the different sections persist; NUG does not have any one leader who can be accepted by the entire nation. This is one reason why outsiders find it difficult to support the Spring Revolution.

Burma's resistance movement against the Myanmar military rule will continue and the process for united efforts of various resistance groups and entities will continue as well. It takes time, patience and political wisdom. The Spring Revolution has shown that more than 50 per cent of country's territories have been liberated from the rule of Myanmar military in the last four and half years which was achieved with a little support from outside but largely by the Burmese inside and outside the country.

The international community can lessen the pain and suffering of our people if they provided humanitarian assistance and effectively sanctioned the military junta.

Is there any way for civil society in the West or in India to extend its solidarity to Myanmar?

Civil society in the West and India can extend solidarity to Myanmar through both direct and indirect support. This includes in areas such as humanitarian aid, diplomatic advocacy, and backing local resistance movements. Specifically, civil society can partner with local groups in the delivery of aid. They can also advocate for targeted sanctions against the military regime, especially against its access to critical supplies like aviation fuel, which is used in bombing campaigns.

Politically, Western and Indian civil society groups can engage with and support Myanmar's National Unity Government (NUG), civil society leaders, and EAOs that are working toward a new federal democracy. This would help to legitimize the resistance and provides a counter-narrative to the junta.

The Burma support groups in different parts of the world can come together for a Coalition of the Willing of Democracies (such as Czech Republic, Sweden, Poland, Ireland, Netherlands, Lithuania, Timor-Leste, Japan, South Korea, Australia, Taiwan, Tibet, Ukraine) to bring the Myanmar cause for democracy and federal union onto the global stage.

The year 2026 should be the year for Myanmar's democracy and federal union with an International Conference on Democracy and Federal Union in Myanmar. It will be good if India can host it as it did in October 2004 in New Delhi.

Indian civil society in particular can further assist in the support of Myanmar refugees in India, providing humanitarian aid and working with local governments to protect the rights and needs and refugee populations. And Indian civil society can also urge the national government to engage with a wider range of non-state actors in Myanmar, better reflecting the ground realities inside Myanmar. Finally, and building on the previous point, Indian civil society can help in raising awareness among the Indian public, political parties, and other civil society groups to shift the Indian government's current approaches toward Myanmar to a stance that more actively supports democratic values in Myanmar.

September 28, 2025

NOTE

1. For the story of *Mizzima* see: Nandita Haksar and Soe Myint, *Resisting Military Rule in Burma (1988-2024): Story of Mizzima Media—Born in Exile, Banned in Myanmar* (Aakar, 2025)

Acknowledgements

My long association with the Burmese refugee community began in 1989 when the first batch of students and protestors crossed into India after the crackdown on the national uprising of 1988. It has been both enrichening experience, politically and personally.

Writing Aung Nay Myo's story gave me a glimpse into the new generation of Burmese who have been exposed to the internet and global trends. Language barriers notwithstanding my interactions with him brought me closer to the Spring Revolution. Thank you Aung Nay Myo and also to your young niece, Nadi Lynn for the lovely meals you cooked for us, especially the crispy pork.

Without the patient and professional translations by Ko Nyo Htun this interaction would have been impossible. Ko Nyo Htun put aside his work with *Mizzima* to help me with the translations and interpretations and I am truly grateful to him and *Mizzima* for their support throughout the writing of this book.

My heartfelt thank you to Divya Kapur for introducing me to Ambika Nair who has not just edited the book but been a moral support for this book.

I am excited by the fact that this book will also be simultaneously be published by Daraja Press in Canada. My heartfelt thanks to both Feroze Manji and Amrit Wilson for making this possible. The cover design of the Canada edition has been done by Min Min Han, a Burmese designer based in the USA.

It has been a pleasure working with K.K. Saxena and his team at Aakar. He has been available at all times and brought out this book in record time.

This book would not have been possible without the personal support and love from Soe Myint and Sebastian.

Annex

Transcript: Aung San Suu Kyi's Speech at the ICJ in Full[1]

In her opening statement in front of judges in The Hague rejected the case at the United Nations' highest court—which was filed by the Gambia with the support of the 57-member Organisation of Islamic Cooperation (OIC)—alleging Myanmar violated the 1948 Convention on the Prevention and Punishment of the Crime of Genocide.

Here is her speech in full:

"Thank you, Mr President and members of the court. It is an honour to appear as Agent of the Union of the Republic of Myanmar in these proceedings, in my capacity as Union Minister of Foreign Affairs.

"For materially less resourceful countries like Myanmar, the World Court is a vital refuge of international justice. We look to the Court to establish conditions conducive to respect for obligations arising from treaties and other sources of international law, one of the fundamental objectives of the United Nations Charter.

"In the present case, Mr President, the Court has been asked to apply the 1948 Genocide Convention, one of the most fundamental multilateral treaties of our time. Invoking the 1948 Genocide Convention is a matter of utmost gravity. This is the treaty that we made following the systematic killing of more than six million European Jews, and that my country wholeheartedly signed as early as December 30, 1949, and ratified on March 14, 1956. Genocide is the crime that the International Criminal Tribunal for Rwanda applied in response to the mass-killing of perhaps 70 per cent of the Tutsis in Rwanda. It is the crime that was not applied by the Tribunal for the former Yugoslavia to the displacement of approximately one million residents of Kosovo in 1999. Neither was it applied by that Tribunal nor by this Court when deciding upon the exodus of the Serb population from Croatia in 1995.

"In both situations, international justice resisted the temptation to use this strongest of legal classifications because the requisite specific intent to physically destroy the targeted group in whole or in part was not present.

"Regrettably, The Gambia has placed before the Court an incomplete and misleading factual picture of the situation in Rakhine State in Myanmar. Yet, it is of the utmost importance that the Court assess the situation obtaining on the ground in Rakhine dispassionately and accurately. The situation in Rakhine is complex and not easy to fathom.

"But one thing surely touches all of us equally: the sufferings of the many innocent people whose lives were torn apart as a consequence of the armed conflicts of 2016 and 2017, in particular, those who have had to flee their homes and are now living in camps in Cox's Bazar.

"Mr President and members of the court, the troubles of Rakhine State and its population, whatever their background, go back into past centuries and have been particularly severe over the last few years. Currently, an internal armed conflict is going on there—between the Arakan Army, an organised Buddhist armed group with more than 5,000 fighters, and the regular Myanmar Defence Services. None of the speakers yesterday made any reference to this.

"The Arakan Army seeks autonomy or independence for Rakhine—or Arakan as it was called—finding inspiration in the memory of the historic Kingdom of Arakan. This conflict has led to the displacement of thousands of civilians in Rakhine. Standard security restrictions—such as curfew and checkpoints—are in place at present in the conflict zone and affect the situation of civilians there, regardless of their background.

"Mr President, on October 9, 2016, approximately 400 fighters of the Arakan Rohingya Salvation Army—known as ARSA—launched simultaneous attacks on three police posts in Maungdaw and Rathedaung townships in northern Rakhine, near the border with Bangladesh. ARSA claimed responsibility for these attacks, which led to the death of nine police officers, more than 100 dead or missing civilians, and the theft of 68 guns and more than 10,000 rounds of ammunition.

"This was the start of an internal armed conflict between ARSA and Myanmar's Defence Services which lasted until late 2017. The selective factual propositions contained in The Gambia's Application actually concern this conflict.

"In the months following the October 9, 2016 attacks, ARSA grew in strength in the Maungdaw, Buthidaung and Rathedaung townships in northern Rakhine. It resorted to threats and intimidation against local villagers in order to gain support and allegiance, executing suspected informers. According to, among others, the International Crisis Group, ARSA received weapons—and explosives—training from Afghan and Pakistani militants.

"In the early morning of August 25, 2017, several thousand ARSA fighters launched coordinated attacks on more than 30 police posts and villages, and an army base in northern Rakhine. Most of the attacks took place on the narrow Maungdaw plain, which is framed by densely forested hills to the east, and the border with Bangladesh to the west. Indications are that ARSA's objective was to seize Maungdaw township.

"It may aid the Court to briefly consider the historical significance of Maungdaw. When Britain made Burma a colonial entity separate from British India in 1937, the border between Burma and India was drawn along the river Naf, where we find today's border between Bangladesh and Myanmar. The historical Kingdom of Arakan had extended much further to the north than the river Naf, including most of what is today Chittagong District in Bangladesh.

"Members of some Rakhine communities, therefore, felt that the border drawn by the British was too far south; others, that it was too far north. Myanmar has never challenged this border since independence in 1948.

"Britain did not lose control over what is today Maungdaw township during World War II. From September 1942, a number of local Muslim families offered fighters to the British irregular V-Force set up to collect intelligence and to initially absorb any Japanese advance. Many Muslims gave their lives in combat against the Japanese in Rakhine.

"The sacrifices made by Muslim fighters motivated a call for the creation of an autonomous Muslim space in northern Rakhine, centred on Maungdaw. Whether or not this was encouraged by British officers, Britain rejected this call as soon as it had reoccupied Burma, before independence in 1948. The Muslim-Buddhist intercommunal violence of 1942 recurred in 1948 and several times after that. This cycle of violence has negatively affected life in northern Rakhine, making it the second poorest state in Myanmar.

"Mr President and members of the court, may I go back to the situation in Rakhine on the morning of August 25, 2017. More than thirty police stations and villages, and one military base, had been attacked before sunrise in a highly coordinated fashion, by an organized armed group operating along a densely forested hill-range that provides ample opportunity to hide. Many of the ARSA fighters had been recruited from local villages in the weeks and months preceding the attack.

"Myanmar's Defence Services responded to the attacks of ARSA fighters by the use of ground forces. There were armed incidents in more than 60 locations. The main clashes occurred in 12 places: In Min Gyi (Tola Toli) village, Chut Pyin village, Maung Nu village, Gutar Pyin village, Alai Than Kyaw village, Myin Lut village, Inn Din village, Chein Kharli (Koetan Kauk) village, Myo Thugyi ward, Kyauk Pandu village, wards of Maungdaw Town, and southern Maungdaw.

"Mr President, allow me to clarify the use of the term 'clearance operation'—'nae myay shin lin yeh' in Myanmar [language]. Its meaning has been distorted. As early as the 1950s, this term has been used during military operations against the Burma Communist Party in Bago Range. Since then, the military has used this expression in counter-insurgency and counter-terrorism operations after attacks by insurgents or terrorists. In the Myanmar language, 'nae myay shin lin yeh'—literally 'clearing of locality'—simply means to clear an area of insurgents or terrorists.

"It is still not easy to establish clear patterns of events in these 12 locations. Many ARSA fighters died. There may have been several hundred casualties in some of the 12 locations. There was some inter-communal violence. Buddhist and Hindu minority communities also feared for their security after the original ARSA attacks and many fled from their homes.

"It may be worth noting that the use of air power in military operations was avoided as far as possible to minimise the risk of collateral damage. However, in one incident, in order to be able to extract a unit surrounded by hundreds of ARSA fighters, the use of a helicopter was required. There was shooting from the helicopter which resulted in fatalities, which may have included noncombatants.

"Mr President, it cannot be ruled out that disproportionate force was used by members of the Defence Services in some cases in disregard of international humanitarian law, or that they did not distinguish clearly enough between ARSA fighters and civilians. There may also have been failures to prevent civilians from looting or destroying property after fighting or in abandoned villages. But these are determinations to be made in the due course of the criminal justice process, not by any individual in the Myanmar Government.

"Please bear in mind this complex situation and the challenge to sovereignty and security in our country when you are assessing the intent of those who attempted to deal with the rebellion. Surely, under the circumstances, genocidal intent cannot be the only hypothesis.

"Under its 2008 Constitution, Myanmar has a military justice system. Criminal cases against soldiers or officers for possible war crimes committed in Rakhine must be investigated and prosecuted by that system. On November 25, 2019, the Office of the Judge Advocate General announced the start of a court-martial for allegations linked to the Gutar Pyin village incident, one of the 12 main incidents referred to earlier. The Office also let it be known that there will be additional courts-martial if further incriminating evidence is brought by the Independent Commission of Enquiry. The ICOE is an independent special investigation procedure established for Rakhine allegations by the President of Myanmar, chaired by a former Deputy Foreign Minister from the Philippines, with three other members, including a former Under-Secretary-General of the United Nations from Japan.

"On November 26, 2019, this Commission announced that it had taken about 1,500 witness statements from all affected groups in Rakhine and that it has interviewed 29 military personnel who were deployed to the affected townships in northern Rakhine during the military operations from August 25, 2017, to September 5, 2017, as well as 20 police personnel who were stationed at the police posts that were attacked on August 25, 2017. There is currently no other fact-finding body in the world that has garnered relevant first-hand information on what occurred in Rakhine in 2017 to the same extent as the Independent Commission of Enquiry and the Office of the Judge Advocate General in Myanmar.

"This fact reinforces my sense that I should refrain from any action or statement that could undermine the integrity of these ongoing criminal justice processes in Myanmar. They must be allowed to run their course. It is never easy for armed forces to recognise self-interest in accountability for their members, and to implement a will to accountability through actual investigations and prosecutions. I respectfully invite the members of the court to consider for a moment the record of other countries. This is a common challenge, even in resource-rich countries.

"Recent cases in the news headlines illustrate that even when military justice works, there can be reversals. This can also happen in Myanmar. As part of the overall efforts of the Myanmar Government to provide justice, a court-martial found that 10 Muslim men had been summarily executed in Inn Din village, one of the 12 locations of serious incidents referred to earlier. It sentenced four officers and three soldiers each to ten years in prison with hard labour. After serving a part of their sentences, they were given a military pardon. Many of us in Myanmar were unhappy with this pardon.

"Other cases are undertaken without controversy. In

the Mansi case, for example, a court-martial sat close to the location in Kachin state where three internally displaced civilians were killed. It sentenced six soldiers, each to 10 years in prison, in January 2018. Relatives of the victims and local civil society representatives were invited to the sentencing.

"The Office of the Judge Advocate General in Myanmar is by our standards well-resourced, with more than 90 staff and a presence in all regional commands throughout the country. I am encouraged by the Gutar Pyin court-martial, and I expect the Office to continue its investigations and prosecutions based on reliable evidence collected in Rakhine and from persons who witnessed what happened there.

"Can there be genocidal intent on the part of a state that actively investigates, prosecutes and punishes soldiers and officers who are accused of wrongdoing? Although the focus here is on members of the military, I can assure you that appropriate action will also be taken against civilian offenders, in line with due process. There will be no tolerance of human rights violations in the Rakhine, or elsewhere in Myanmar.

"Mr President, there are those who wish to externalise accountability for alleged war crimes committed in Rakhine, almost automatically, without proper reflection. Some of the United Nations human rights mandates relied upon in the Application presented by The Gambia have even suggested that there cannot be accountability through Myanmar's military justice system. This not only contradicts Article 20(b) of the Constitution of Myanmar, it undercuts painstaking domestic efforts relevant to the establishing of cooperation between the military and the civilian government in Myanmar, in the context of a Constitution that needs to be amended to complete the process of democratization. That process is now underway at the Pyidaungsu Hluttaw, the Union Parliament.

"The emerging system of international criminal justice rests on the principle of complementarity. Accountability through domestic criminal justice is the norm. Only if domestic accountability fails, may international justice come into play. It would be inconsistent with complementarity to require that domestic criminal justice should proceed much faster than international criminal justice. A rush to externalise accountability may undermine professionals in domestic criminal justice agencies. What does the appearance of competition between domestic and international accountability do to the public's trust in the intentions of impatient international actors?

"No stone should be left unturned to make domestic accountability work. It would not be helpful for the international legal order if the impression takes hold that only resource-rich countries can conduct adequate domestic investigations and prosecutions, and that the domestic justice of countries still striving to cope with the burden of unhappy legacies and present challenges is not good enough. The Gambia will also understand this challenge with which they too are confronted.

"Mr President and members of the court, these reflections are relevant to the present hearing because the Applicant has brought a case based on the Genocide Convention. We are, however, dealing with an internal armed conflict, started by coordinated and comprehensive attacks by the Arakan Rohingya Salvation Army, to which Myanmar's Defence Services responded. Tragically, this armed conflict led to the exodus of several hundred thousand Muslims from the three northernmost townships of Rakhine into Bangladesh—just as the armed conflict in Croatia with which the Court had to deal led to the massive exodus of, first, ethnic Croats and later, ethnic Serbs.

"As I have already stated, if war crimes have been committed by members of Myanmar's Defence Services, they will be prosecuted through our military justice system, in accordance with Myanmar's Constitution. It is a matter for the competent criminal justice authorities to assess whether, for example, there has been inadequate distinction between civilians and ARSA fighters, disproportionate use of force, violations of human rights, failure to prevent plundering or property destruction, or acts of forcible displacement of civilians. Such conduct, if proven, could be relevant under international humanitarian law or human rights conventions, but not under the 1948 Genocide Convention for reasons Professor William Schabas will elaborate in a moment.

"Mr President, allow me to share one further reflection in this Great Hall of Justice. International law may well be our only global value system, and international justice a practice that affirms our common values. Leaders of States and relevant inter-governmental and non-governmental organisations should also be cognisant of their responsibility to express and affirm fundamental values. Feeding the flames of an extreme polarisation in the context of Rakhine, for example, can harm the values of peace and harmony in Myanmar. Aggravating the wounds of conflict can undermine unity in Rakhine. Hate narratives are not simply confined to hate speech—language that contributes to extreme polarisation also amounts to hate narratives.

"Several international actors face a challenge here. But Myanmar could also have done more since the 1980s to emphasise the shared heritage and deeper layers of unity among the diverse peoples of our country. Cycles of inter-communal violence in Rakhine going back to the 1940s should be countered not just by practical measures aimed at sustainable development and rule of law, but also by nourishing a spiritual mindset of unity. It is a moral responsibility of leaders to guard the aspirations of people for harmony and peace.

"U Thant, the third United Nations Secretary-General, had understood this. He wrote in his memoirs View From the UN published in 1974: 'I even believe that the mark of the truly educated and imaginative person facing the twenty-first century is that he feels himself to be anetary citizen' (p. 454). Encouraging this added layer cf identity—a sense of planetary citizenship—is of fundamental importance for peaceful relations between nations as well as ethnic and religious groups.

"A commitment to broadening the mindset must go hand in hand with practical steps to improve lives. Even before the events of 2016-17, Muslim, Buddhist and other communities in Rakhine faced what the Kofi Annan Advisory Commission described as complex challenges of low development and poverty rooted in enduring social conflict between the communities. The Myanmar government is committed to addressing these challenges. Together with our partners, we are now striving to ensure that all communities enjoy the same fundamental rights. To expedite citizenship verification and application, a mobile team is already in operation.

"All children born in Rakhine, regardless of religious background, are issued with birth certificates. Arrangements have been made to enable more Muslim youth to attend classes at universities across Myanmar. With the support of international and local partners, scholarships will also be made available to students from all communities living in Rakhine. The government has started a social cohesion model project in Maungdaw township, to promote social harmony among all communities. Inter-faith fora have been encouraged.

"These are some of the steps taken to improve liveli-hoods, security, access to education and health, citizenship, and social cohesion for all communities in Rakhine. Three IDP camps have already been closed, and an IDP-camp closure strategy has been adopted. Myanmar is also committed to voluntary, safe and dignified repatriation of displaced persons from Rakhine under the framework agreement reached between Bangladesh and Myanmar.

"Mr President, how can there be an ongoing genocide or genocidal intent when these concrete steps are being taken in Rakhine?

"To conclude, Mr President and members of the court, Rakhine today suffers an internal armed conflict between the Buddhist Arakan Army and Myanmar's Defence Services. Muslims are not a party to this conflict, but may, like other civilians in the conflict area, be affected by security measures that are in place. We pray the Court to refrain from taking any action that might aggravate the ongoing armed conflict and peace and security in Rakhine. Right now, in northern Rakhine, an army base near Paletwa is under attack by a group of more than 400 Arakan Army fighters, and some 200 insurgents have surrounded a military column near Ann City in Rakhine.

"Since Myanmar gained independence in 1948, our people have not known the security of sustainable development that is the fruit of peace and prosperity. Our greatest challenge is to address the roots of distrust and fear, prejudice and hate, that undermine the foundations of our Union. We shall adhere steadfastly to our commitment to non-violence, human rights, national reconciliation and rule of law, as we go forward to build the Democratic Federal Union to which our people have aspired for generations past.

"We look to justice as a champion of the reconciliation and harmony that will assure the security and rights of all peoples.

"Mr President and members of the court, I thank you for your kind attention and ask that you now call upon Professor William Schabas to continue the Myanmar submissions."

NOTE

1. https://www.aljazeera.com/news/2019/12/12/transcript-
   aung-san-suu-kyis-speech-at-the-icj-in-full Published On 12 Dec
   2019

About the Author

Nandita Haksar (b 1954) is a human rights lawyer, campaigner and teacher. She has taken up cases on behalf of adivasis, workers, and religious minority workers. Haksar has been associated with the Burmese resistance movement since 1988, when there was a national uprising followed by a military crackdown, which forced Burmese students and activists to take shelter in India.

As a human rights lawyer, she has fought cases on behalf of Burmese refugees and continues to do so as more refugees flee to India from Myanmar. In the process, she has set important precedents in refugee law.

Haksar is the author of more than 20 books, including her latest, co-authored with Burmese journalist Soe Myint, titled *Resisting Military Rule in Burma (1988-2024): The Story of Mizzima Media – Born in Exile, Banned in Myanmar* (2025).

Her writings have earned her numerous awards for her contributions to peace in conflict areas.

EU Safety Information

Publisher: Daraja Press, PO Box 99900 BM 735 664 Wakefield, QC J0X 0C2, Canada

info@darajapress.com | https://darajapress.com

EU Authorized GPSR Representative: Easy Access System Europe – Mustamäe tee 50, 10621 Tallinn, Estonia, gpsr.requests@easproject.com

For EU product safety concerns, please contact us at info@darajapress.com

www.ingramcontent.com/pod-product-compliance
Lightning Source LLC
Chambersburg PA
CBHW061807120626
46550CB00005B/2176